MONEY OFF THE TABLE

MONEY OFF THE TABLE

DECISION SCIENCE AND THE
SECRET TO SMARTER INVESTING

TONY SABLAN, AIF, MBA
—— *and* ——
NIKA KABIRI, JD, PHD

HOUNDSTOOTH
PRESS

COPYRIGHT © 2020 TONY SABLAN & NIKA KABIRI

MONEY OFF THE TABLE
Decision Science and the Secret to Smarter Investing

ISBN 978-1-5445-1690-5 *Hardcover*
    978-1-5445-1689-9 *Paperback*
    978-1-5445-1688-2 *Ebook*

For Lucian.

May all your dreams come true.

CONTENTS

DISCLAIMER

This material is presented for informational purposes only and represents our understanding of generally applicable rules. It is not intended and does not set forth solutions to individual situations. Tony Sablan or Nika Kabiri may not give legal, tax, or accounting advice, and none is intended nor should be inferred from the information herein. Readers should consult their own professional advisors before implementing any planning strategies.

This material includes a discussion of one or more tax-related topics that are not intended (and cannot be used by any taxpayer) for the purpose of avoiding any IRS penalties that may be imposed upon the taxpayer. Neither Tony Sablan nor Nika Kabiri provide legal or tax advice. You are urged to consult your legal and tax advisors regarding your particular situation.

INTRODUCTION

Everything you need to know about investing is already out there. "Gurus" on TV will tell you what stocks to buy. Websites can explain what bonds and annuities are. Wealth advisors can offer strategic help. Sometimes you have to hunt for it, but the information you need already exists.

It's as if the world doesn't need another book about investing.

But if this is true, then tell me, why aren't more people retiring earlier? Why are some investors winning while others are losing? Why aren't more people leaving greater inheritances for their children? And most of all, why do so many investors have a nagging feeling about whether or not they're doing the right thing?

All of my clients come to me with some knowledge about

investing. On one end, there are investors who only have a 401K. On the other end, there are people with millions of dollars invested in a variety of vehicles, from stocks to real estate to annuities to cryptocurrency. Some have been investing for months; others for years. In short, they run the gamut.

One thing I've noticed while working with these investors is that knowledge does not correlate with success. People who read all the right books and meet with multiple advisors, who use all the right jargon and keep on top of the latest news, can still have huge gaps in their investment plans, leaving them vulnerable and less wealthy than they could be. Meanwhile, people with little investment experience can be set up for success.

It becomes hard, after a while, to avoid the inevitable conclusion that there's more to investing than just knowledge. This book is about "something more"—that extra element you need beyond knowledge to increase the likelihood of success.

That "something more" is the right mindset.

Uncertainty in Investing

Making the right investment decisions is not easy. It's stressful and full of uncertainty. With most purchase decisions in life—like which brand of potato chips to buy, which car to get, or which laptop your kid should have—you have a decent shot at weighing the pros and cons of the purchase because you know what to expect. Potato chips won't become corn chips once you open the bag. A black sedan won't become a white truck once you drive it off the lot.

Investing is different. Your investments could perform exactly the same two years from now as they do today, or they could drop (or rise) dramatically in value. Even the strongest stocks are susceptible to volatility; recent history has shown this to be true.

Investing in real estate isn't a sure thing either, despite the commonly held belief that property values always increase. Sure, many types of investments eventually go up over time, but where will they be the moment you need to cash them in? How will they be performing on the day of your retirement? This you can't predict. Anyone who says they can predict the market is brashly overconfident, in denial, or one of very few wealthy people who can change market performance just by dumping a lot of stock.

I often tell prospective clients who say they can predict the market that they should quit their jobs and start negotiating a seven-figure salary with a top financial firm. No one takes me up on it. The uncertainty inherent in investing can do wacky things to peoples' mindsets. Some investors become way too confident, over-compensating for their lack of certainty with bold decisions backed by force of will. Others lose confidence altogether, succumbing to the advice of slick salespeople with their own agendas.

Having tons of knowledge and experience doesn't make you immune to uncertainty. As long as uncertainty can enter the picture, so will bad decision-making.

This is no one's fault. It's part of being human. Our brains aren't computers. They aren't designed to handle complex calculations involving multiple data points. They're influenced by emotion and physiology. They can only absorb and process a limited amount of information, and oftentimes, information isn't easily accessible. To top it off, humans are social creatures: we care about what others think and how our behavior is interpreted. We're also creatures of habit, learning from our institutions and our culture about what's right and what's wrong, what's smart and what's not, and going along with social "rules" because they're expected.

And we can't predict the future—even computers can't do that.

When we're faced with decisions under conditions of uncertainty, like the decisions we make in investing, we're bound to make choices that don't always lead us in the right direction.

What This Book Is About

This book will give you information that's missing in other books today: information designed to help protect you from the flaws of your own decision-making so you can be confident in your investment choices, no matter the situation you're in, and no matter how the market is performing. Using knowledge from behavioral and social science about decision-making under uncertainty, the information in this book will help you do a better job of avoiding bad choices that may cause you to lose money. It will also help you build good practices that can decrease the likelihood of financial loss, even in volatile times.

If you've found yourself feeling insecure about getting started with investing, then this book is for you. If you're a seasoned investor feeling shaky about your portfolio, or you have a funny feeling that you could do better, then this book is also for you. If you feel good about your investment decisions but just want to cover your bases, then you should also read this book.

If you want to learn what an annuity or money market account is, then read another book. That kind of information exists pretty much everywhere else. Here, you'll learn *how to think about the information you have*, and how to adjust your mindset so that your decision-making is more confident and lucrative.

And in the end, with the market being what it is, *real confidence* is what matters the most.

CHAPTER 1

RUDE AWAKENING

At twenty-three, I was a rock star investor. A wealth management prodigy. A whiz kid and a badass.

At least that's what I felt like. For a little while.

I had landed a well-paying consulting job at a boutique firm, one that came with a SEP-IRA and the freedom to invest my contributions however I wanted. Given my humble beginnings, this was an incredible accomplishment. I grew up on a tiny little island north of Guam called Saipan, where my parents ran an import/export business. I was one of five kids raised by my mom, for the most part. My father died shortly before I turned sixteen, and he didn't leave much, so we didn't have much. We had no life insurance. No investments. No savings.

Overnight, we went from being upper middle class to lower

class, barely scraping by. In the following years, I watched my mom work day and night to provide for us. She taught me the value of working hard and saving money.

So, achieving the job and investment opportunities I had at the young age of twenty-three was a really big deal.

After four years of working at the boutique firm, I had $60,000 in my retirement account and a portfolio that had gained 20 percent. My portfolio was hardly diverse: it consisted of exclusively tech and financial services stocks, and one oil company tossed in for good measure. At the time, tech and financial services were all the rage on the financial soap operas (you know, Bloomberg, CNBC, *The Wall Street Journal*). I had no mutual funds and no life insurance except for what was handed to me by my company.

Because my portfolio wasn't diverse, it was risky. But that didn't bother me. It didn't have to. My amazing returns spoke for themselves, and I figured that without risk there would be no reward. Tuning in daily to a portfolio that I thought was going to keep growing over the next forty years was exciting. It didn't matter to me that I was surrounded by information warning against my strategy. I believed in myself and in the results. I believed I was onto a better way.

I believed I was a hot shot. Yeah... I was *that* guy.

Around that time, I was at a local networking event and found myself chatting with one of the presenters—an experienced financial advisor. He asked me if I'd be willing to sit down with him. "I'd like to show you what I do," he said calmly.

I was reluctant. I mean, I didn't *need* him to show me what he did. I already knew what I was doing. But not wanting to be rude, I said, "OK."

He asked me to describe my financial picture, my hopes and dreams, and my retirement goals. Then he asked me to give him a little time.

A week later, he came back with a financial plan that was custom-tailored to my situation. It seemed comprehensive and well thought out, but it was dull, and the returns weren't impressive. He suggested I purchase whole life insurance as part of my overall portfolio of assets.

I thought, *"But I'm too young to worry about life insurance."*

He also advised me to re-allocate my funds across a more diversified portfolio.

I said to myself, *"Why would I do that when my current choices are so hot?"*

He showed me my projected earnings. According to him,

if I followed his plan, which was based on what I told him about my goals, I would retire before age forty.

I still wasn't convinced. Trusting my gut, I concluded that his plan just wasn't right for me. I believed I could do better.

I told him thanks, but no thanks.

I slept well making that decision. Well, for a year anyway.

The Fallout—Losing 40 Percent of My Portfolio Overnight

That next year, I went on vacation. I was still earning a lot from my investments, and I decided to enjoy some of the money by spending it on travel and visiting a friend who lived in Thailand. In the daytime, we lounged at the beach and went shopping. In the evenings, we went out to dinner. Late at night, we hit the bar and club scene. Each day, I checked my stocks online and saw that my earnings were healthy. I was living the dream: getting wealthy, traveling, and enjoying the fruits of my smart decisions. I thought I was onto a formula that few others knew about. I truly believed I had it all figured out. And, dare I say it, I thought I was special.

Until...

About halfway through my trip, while going through my

routine of stopping by an internet café, buying a cup of coffee, logging on to Wi-Fi, and checking my stocks, my whole world changed. Like every other day, I expected to see great returns. I expected to see evidence of my success so I could pat myself on the back, prove to myself once again how brilliant I was, and smugly make my way back to the beach.

But on that particular day, when I saw the numbers, I lost my breath. In one day, my stock values had plummeted, and 40 percent of my earnings were gone.

Just like that.

I did a double take. And a triple take. I thought I read the numbers wrong. Maybe it was all a glitch, and if I just refreshed the page enough times it would change.

But it didn't.

Suddenly, reality set in. My perfect vacation became sullied by panic.

Meanwhile, all across America, many others like me were having the exact same experience. It was the early 2000s, when the stock market dipped dramatically, and many Americans lost the bulk of their investments. Between January 1, 2001, and September 24, 2002, the Dow Jones lost a total of $5 trillion. Just when the market looked like it had recovered, along came the Great Recession of 2008. People lost their homes, their retirement savings, and their hopes for a comfortable future. What once seemed like a sure thing suddenly became profoundly uncertain.

And no one saw it coming.

When Uncertainty Hits, are You Passive, Reactive, or a Little Bit of Both?

People often say investing is like gambling. The recession made this sentiment hit home. There is no crystal ball, even though we badly want it to be a sure thing. No matter what financial pundits say on TV or on the internet, there are no guarantees. The market can plummet, or it can thrive. There's no way to predict it.

Some people react to this uncertainty by being passive and not taking the time to make thoughtful or strategic investment decisions. They put some money into their 401K because their employer puts a 401K in front of them. They might have some company stock, but again, for no other reason than their employer putting that stock in front of them or giving it as a reward. They might buy a house because they were told that's what they should eventually do. And then they just sit back and hope for the best.

Other people go the other way and react to uncertainty by being impulsive. They take huge risks because uncertainty feels crappy, and taking dramatic action makes them (temporarily) feel in control. These folks might be way too overconfident or optimistic. They truly believe that if they take a huge risk, they'll get rich fast. The fact that get-rich-quick investments *sometimes* work gives them the courage to try. But they don't *always* work. In fact, they fail more often than not. But this doesn't matter to impulsive investors; they're so focused on the potential wins that they're blind to potential losses.

Not everyone will be passive or reactive. Some people might just follow what their friends do, what investment celebrities tell them to do, or even follow what they hear through the grapevine. They don't think strategically or prepare for contingencies. They make decisions, but their decisions go along with the flow, even when the "flow" isn't moving in the right direction for them.

There are so many ways in which people can make poor investment decisions. In my experience as a wealth advisor, I feel like I've seen it all, and many of these poor choices were made by people with a lot of experience. Limited knowledge and experience have nothing to do with making bad decisions. Being human is the problem.

You're not totally at the mercy of the market, and you will

never build a portfolio with guarantees, but with the right mindset, you can build a portfolio that can optimize your chances of retiring on financially solid ground. Mindset is everything. If you have the right mindset, you can feel confident in your investment decisions. To get the right mindset, you must accept the fact that while uncertain, you're going to make some crappy decisions. Then, set up some guardrails to protect yourself from yourself. In other words, recognize you're human, and then override your *human* tendencies when they don't work for you.

It sounds difficult, but it's easier than you think. If you really care about your financial future, and the future of your family, this is worth a shot.

And I'll tell you exactly how to do it.

The Turnaround—How I got Radically Open-Minded about My Situation and Developed the Right Mindset

Back in Thailand, after the market had tanked and I lost much of my earnings, I made a few minor adjustments to my portfolio. I sold some of my assets, which made me feel better because I felt like I did *something*. I closed my laptop and decided that the dip was temporary and that everything would soon even out. I decided that, worst-case scenario, my retirement would come later than I thought. Not ideal, but I'd be fine.

I walked to the beach, ordered a drink, laid in the sun, and put it out of my mind.

But every day after that, for many days, I checked my portfolio and saw no recovery. I kept trying to convince myself that I knew what I was doing; the market would course-correct and I'd be back on track. But it didn't happen. And as time went on, I felt less and less hopeful.

Then I realized I had to get real. No matter what I thought I knew, or how smart I thought I was, something wasn't quite right. I'd lost confidence. I faced the fact that I wasn't the investment hot shot I thought I was. I was wrong in believing that the market would quickly adjust to where it was before. I was wrong in thinking the best course of action was to sell a few stocks and wait it out.

I had to get radically open-minded about my situation.

And my situation was this: I had all the information I needed. I knew about diversifying and re-allocating. A year earlier, a seasoned wealth advisor had given me a plan that would have increased my likelihood of seeing steady, long-term growth.

I basically had, in my hands, the blueprint for a smart investment strategy, but I rejected it. I didn't think the rules applied to me because I believed I had all the facts.

But I didn't have the right mindset. And in the end, that's what really counted.

It was rough to admit that I hadn't been facing reality. Rude awakenings are called "rude" for a reason. But with eyes widely opened and my ego thoroughly humbled, I finally reached out for help.

It was then that a good friend recommended I talk to his financial advisor. I made an appointment and hoped his help would get me on track. When I met with him, it felt like fate. As it happened, he was the same guy I had met at that networking event some time ago—the one who drew me a custom-tailored plan that optimized my chances of retiring by age forty.

You know the plan...the one I turned down. Because it was dull and unexciting, and because I knew so much better.

But this time, I was open. He set me up with a diverse portfolio, one more resistant to unexpected market fluctuations than the one I had. He signed me up for whole life insurance that would grow to where, by the time I had a family, they'd be provided for in case times got tough, or if I didn't make it home one day. He didn't try to impress me with promises of high returns, quick results, or guaranteed earnings.

But most importantly, he reset my mindset.

He educated me on why certain assets should be in place, and how each asset acts differently in different situations. Most importantly, he provided me with a holistic plan that took life's ups and downs into account.

As he explained to me why I needed to invest in the assets he recommended, it dawned on me that it wasn't my knowledge that failed me. It was the way that I had been processing that knowledge. I had been *acting* confident in my investment decisions, but my decisions weren't made with real confidence at all.

That moment was the start of a growth journey that continues to this day. This journey has led me to gather incredible insights about how people approach investing and how they make investment decisions. It led me to become a wealth advisor so I could help other people create holistic plans with the right mindset. It has driven me to understand why so many people—all with access to so much information about investing—could get it wrong. Including me.

My journey also led me to share my thoughts and experiences with my friend and co-author Nika Kabiri, JD PhD, a social scientist who has spent over twenty years studying human decision-making in a variety of contexts, and who teaches Decision Science at the University of Washington. Through my conversations with her, I came to understand that at the core of the investor's mindset lies the problem of uncertainty, and that when human beings are faced with uncertainty, their brains can perform in sub-optimal ways. Even without uncertainty, our brains can lead us in the wrong direction. If we can identify when, how, and why we go astray; be mindful enough to override our less-than-ideal decision-making tendencies, and establish a plan to protect us from our imperfections, we can make much better decisions.

This is true of all decisions we make in life, and it's definitely true about investing.

The only reason I'm not destitute today is because I made a choice to let go of my old mindset. I chose to be radically aware of the basic human tendencies that lead to errors in judgment. I chose to be on the lookout for the many social pressures that influence human decision-making.

Today, I no longer care about being "a badass" or "a genius." I work hard to ignore the noise of social pressure and normative expectations. I pay attention to how my limited brainpower forces me to take mental shortcuts and succumb to biases, and how my emotions sometimes get the best of me. Instead of using hubris to cope with the stress of uncertainty, I work to get real about my options and their consequences, which has opened me up to making better choices with confidence.

And now Nika and I want to share what we know.

What's to Come In These Uncertain Times

Our global economy is experiencing unprecedented times. It's never been so important to understand not just how the markets work and how to invest in them, but also how our brains work so we can invest wisely.

In the next chapter, you'll learn how research in the social sciences informs the study of human decision-making and how this research applies to personal investing. You'll learn about decision-making pitfalls that happen at the individual level: pitfalls that stem from limitations of the human brain, as well as psychological, physical, and emotional influences that sway how choices are made. You'll also learn about pitfalls that stem from social influences, like how our culture and social interactions limit us by telling us what's acceptable or possible.

While Chapter 2 delivers the bad news—the many ways in which our decision-making can let us down—Chapter 3 delivers the good news: solid advice to help make sure that bad decision-making doesn't compromise your investments.

Chapters 4 through 8 cover common examples of investment mindsets that can send decision-making in a bad direction. You'll learn how each example illustrates problematic decision-making, the mindset that causes the problem, and how to fix it. By the end of this book, you'll know some major ways in which investors make bad decisions, and you'll be armed with solutions to help avoid making them yourself.

Nika and I hope that with the guidance provided in this book, you can feel confident you've embraced the necessary mindset and strategy to increase the chances of financial success for you and your family.

The market may throw a few curve balls, and some might be nasty, but if you invest confidently, you increase your chances of being okay. There are no guarantees and there is no crystal ball. But given the opportunity to dramatically increase your chances of success, why not take it?

CHAPTER 2

WE DON'T MAKE THE BEST DECISIONS

The reason I made bad investment decisions when I was younger is because I didn't have the right mindset. What's the right mindset? Let's start by describing the *wrong* mindset.

The wrong mindset leads one to believe that a decision that *feels* right is actually right. The wrong mindset allows the ego to make decisions because it wants us to be someone we don't need to be. The wrong mindset doesn't care about our mental, physical, and emotional wellness, and it doesn't care to question the choices we make out of routine—the choices we make because, well...it's just what's always been done.

In contrast, the right mindset starts with accepting the fact that, by being human, we are automatically susceptible to making decisions that don't always get us to where we want to be. There's no judgment here. It's part of the human condition that the same decision-making that leads us to great places can also lead us to some not-so-great places. When you embrace the right investment mindset, you're aware that if you're not careful, it could go the wrong way.

The right mindset also involves awareness that our social and cultural environments influence our decision-making—often without our acknowledgement. Influence is always there, pushing us in one direction and pulling us in another. There are influences all around us: society and culture tell us what's expected and what various behaviors mean for our reputations and our ability to belong. But there are also influences *within* us: our psychology and physiology, if uncared for, can hinder our ability to accurately weigh outcomes, making us more comfortable with risk than we should be. The right mindset acknowledges that these things happen as we make decisions, pretty much all the time.

Once we admit that our decision-making is perpetually "under the influence," and as long as we are open to looking out for those influences, we are well on our way. But the right mindset also involves a third element: a commitment to circumventing these influences, or at least lessening their impact. It's not enough to think to yourself, "As I make this decision, I am influenced by peer pressure, familial obligations, or my inability to think straight due to lack of sleep." You must *do* something about it.

But first, let's get into what could happen if you aren't aware, and how things can so easily go wrong.

Being Unaware Can Cost You Money

Before I reset my investment mindset, I was unaware of how my mind, emotions, and environment forced me to take mental shortcuts, rely on biases, or use my gut to make decisions—especially when my gut turned out to be wrong. I didn't pay attention to how my stress and anxiety led to risky investment choices, especially as I started to notice my earnings slide. I didn't realize how much I cared about how others perceived me, to where I craved an identity centered on wealth and success at the expense of my actual earnings. And I wasn't aware that the investment information and advice I was getting came from a group of close-knit friends and associates who thought exactly like I did, closing me off from other types of information I really needed.

Because I wasn't aware, I'm not where I wanted to be in my life right now. I wanted to be much closer to retirement than I am. I wanted my son's savings account to be larger than it is. I wanted to have more money to pass on to my son when I die so he could retire early, or maybe not even feel the pressure to work at all.

The wrong mindset cost me, and it cost my family.

These days, I'm OK with this, because I also recognize that my poor judgment is part of being human. I can forgive myself for that. As Nika often says, "If we lived in a perfect world, we'd be perfect too." But the world isn't close to perfect, and as people, we do our best to get by.

Unfortunately, our imperfections, though human and understandable, can sometimes hurt us, leaving us in worse situations than what we really want. We think we're doing all we can to protect ourselves and create the best lives for ourselves, and we try really hard to make all of this happen. But too often, our human limitations and social environments pull us back.

This is not just true with investing. It's true in all aspects of life. We regularly make small and big life decisions without being 100 percent aware of every aspect of our decision-making process. The jobs we choose, the products we buy, the person we marry, whether or not to get a divorce...we try to make these decisions well. But because we're human, we're pushed or pulled toward one decision or another by the many forces at play within us and around us, often without knowing it. The trick is to identify these forces and short-circuit them before they cause too much damage.

Bad decision-making doesn't just happen while investing—it happens all the time. Here are some examples to show you what I mean.

Consider Sandra. She's been working as a personal injury lawyer at a mid-sized firm for five years and is now eager to open her own solo practice. She knows the law and is great at handling cases that senior attorneys hand to her.

But she isn't sure how to get her own clients. What should she do?

What if I told you that Sandra decided to get clients by spending money on advertising—money she really can't afford to spend? She has no market analysis telling her that advertising will bring in the most business for her practice. She chooses to advertise simply because advertising is what many personal injury lawyers do, and if they do it, she concludes, there must be good reason.[1]

So, she hires someone to create a TV ad for her, and she pays a local TV station to air that ad late at night. But business doesn't pick up. She gets some phone calls, but none are from people with cases that could hold up in court. Four months into her new practice and she's already in debt, with no extra funds to pay for a different marketing strategy that might actually work better.

There's also Mariam, whose husband of three years has left her for another woman. Mariam is devastated. Since the split-up two months ago, she's been unable to sleep, has lost the ability to enjoy anything, and spends her weekends in bed. Her sister, concerned, urges Mariam to seek help from a psychologist to help her process the breakup in a healthy way. Her sister even finds a counselor for her and makes an appointment.

The date and time of the appointment approaches, and Mariam isn't sure if she should go. What should she do?

What if I told you Mariam looked up the counselor's professional profile online, and though the profile was appealing, she decided not to go to the appointment? Not because she compared the qualities of that counselor to other options (like seeing a different counselor, or no counselor at all), but because her depression made her feel as though nothing and no one would *ever* make her feel better, so what was the point?[2] And because of this choice, Mariam sunk even deeper into depression, costing her valuable weeks of life that she could have spent living.

And then there's Alec. He and Imani recently moved into a new home together with their Labrador puppy. From the moment they decided to buy a house, Alec felt pummeled by one decision after another: where to buy a home, which specific home to buy, what colors should go on the walls, what furniture they should get, which plumber they should hire to fix the leaky faucet...

One day, Imani showed Alec an expensive rug she found online. They don't need a rug, but she really loves it and asks Alec if they should buy it. He notices the rug is white and really plush, which could be a problem given they have a young dog. They've already been spending so much on the house, but the rug would look amazing in their living room.

What should he do?

What if I told you that Alec bought the rug? Not because he weighed the pros and cons of having the rug against the pros and cons of not having it, but because he was so fatigued by making so many *other* decisions that he simply didn't have it in him to make a good choice anymore.[3] Within a week of buying the rug—you can probably guess—the puppy ruined it.

Sandra, Mariam, and Alec aren't unintelligent, unaware, or reckless. They, like all of us, try hard to make the right decisions. But as humans we experience limitations and constraints, which can be costly if we don't pay attention to them. These stories are examples of how all of us could use knowledge from the study of human decision-making to make better choices and have better life outcomes.

If Sandra, Mariam, and Alec were faced with making investment decisions instead of other life decisions, they would be no less susceptible to the human pitfalls that lead people in the wrong direction. The good news is that, as humans, we possess the capability to override our limitations. Humans can be flawed, but we also have an incredible capacity to be self-aware and mindful, which means we can train ourselves to see pitfalls before we fall into them.

Decision-Making Pitfalls Happen Under the Radar

The right mindset assumes that decision-making pitfalls are always there and are happening under the radar. They can lead us astray in many ways. Each time they strike, they likely do so without our knowledge. No one tries to make a bad decision; we all do our best. But because we're subject to influences that mess with our decision-making, we don't always come out ahead. When it comes to investment decisions, pitfalls in decision-making can cause us to invest in ways that leave us financially vulnerable or that leave money on the table.

As long as these influences aren't apparent to us, we can't protect ourselves against them.

The right investment mindset involves being honest about the fact that no matter how hard you try or how good you feel about your choices, you're bound to be under the influence of some psychological or social force that can lead to a poor choice. Starting out with that assumption will open you up to see what you usually don't see: the forces that push and pull you into bad decision-making.

Once you've reset your mindset to be aware of these forces, you're better able to spot them when they show up. You'll also be able to exercise the power to decide whether or not you *want* them to influence your decisions (rather than having them influence you without your control). Once you know what's influencing you, and you've chosen which influences you want to avoid and which ones you want to keep, you'll be in charge of your decisions, rather than being pushed and pulled by the forces around you.

In short, you'll have more *real* control, and you'll have more confidence.

There are some major influences relevant to investing that can indicate what you need to be mindful of. The more of these influences you can identify as you embrace the right investment mindset, the better off you're likely to be.

Our brains can trick us with shortcuts as we think through

choices. Research in the behavioral sciences reveals many ways in which people take mental shortcuts, known as *heuristics*, and rely on biases when making decisions, rather than evaluating options thoroughly and carefully. Human brains are limited; behavioral economists call this *bounded rationality*.[4] We want to be objective. We try hard to be careful and thoughtful. But given that we're people, we can only do so much, especially when our environments are becoming increasingly complex.

There are too many examples of heuristics and biases to cover in this book, but I've listed a few below. Other examples will show up in later chapters, but don't worry, you don't have to remember them all. You just have to know they exist—you can always refer back to this book to make sure you're on the right track.

Let's start by stating a general rule: if you want to make good decisions, you have to figure out how likely it is for each outcome to occur, as well as how appealing or valuable each outcome is to you. If you're trying to decide between tech stock and energy stock, for example, it helps to know how each are going to perform in the future. To understand how likely it is that something good will happen in a few days, months, or years down the road, you really should do the "math." This means relying on the laws of statistics and the rules of probability.

I know... it sounds painful, but it really is the best way. It's objective, scientific, and rational.

But probability isn't easy to apply every day, especially on the spot. And when we're trying to predict something that's hard to predict (like stock market performance), we can get stuck. In circumstances where doing the "math" takes too much time and energy, and where risks and rewards are hard to estimate, human beings rely on mental shortcuts to make decisions.

One common way we use shortcuts is by looking at *characteristics* of the companies we want to invest in and deciding if those companies seem like ones that would do well in the stock market. This is part of our very human tendency to make connections, even if those connections don't exist.[5]

Have you ever tried to tell a friend about an experience you've had, only to have them interrupt you and say, "That *exact* same thing happened to me! I know *exactly* what you're going through!" Your friend in this example would do better to sit back, listen, take in your entire story, and then ask questions to make sure they understand it completely. However, being human, they quickly spot connections. They hear aspects of your partially-told story that are similar to their own experiences, and they draw conclusions about your situation from partial evidence. But they don't quite get it right because a few similarities aren't enough, and what they think is your story isn't the whole story.

Our Brains Look for Connections that May Not Be There—This Can Be a Problem

Situations like this with friends can feel annoying, but when making investment decisions, the results can be more serious. Some investors think about the attributes of a strong-performing company, and then ask themselves if each company they want to buy stock in is similar to those companies that perform strongly. But just because something walks, talks, and smells like a strong stock doesn't mean it will yield you the strongest returns.

For example, just because major tech companies perform well in the market doesn't mean that investing in an emerging tech company is best for you. You can compare a budding tech company to Microsoft or Amazon in a number of different ways: charismatic CEO, lots of press attention, headquartered in Seattle, and creating new technology. But that doesn't mean that a new Seattle company with a charismatic leader that's featured in *Wired* is worth investing in.

This might be obvious to you now, as you calmly read this book. But when it's time to make a decision, many of us, having too little information, or too little time or interest in thinking strategically, default to efficient but sub-optimal decision-making. It happens under the radar and can come on suddenly. Because, without information or interest in learning more, how else will you make your decision? You decide based on what you already know and on connections you might see.

You can run into trouble if you care too much about similarities between events and care too little about the probability of certain outcomes. How well a company represents itself within a certain category doesn't matter as much as the actual "math." But in investing, when it's so very hard (if not impossible) to look into the future and evaluate the probability of a stock's success, it's easy to fall into the "it walks like a duck" trap.

Also, just because a company has some great traits doesn't mean it's great in all aspects. For example, a coffee company may serve fair trade coffee beans and get public kudos for caring about sustainability, all the while using disposable, non-recyclable coffee cups without even a peep of consumer complaint. A company like this is benefitting from what's called the *halo effect*.[6]

Similarly, if a company carries all the traits of a success story *outside* of the stock market, this doesn't mean it's a sure thing *inside* the stock market. Yet, our biases lead us to believe otherwise, causing us to invest in companies that look great on the surface, but don't operate well financially under the hood. One person interviewed during the writing of this book said they sold a bulk of their stocks so they could concentrate more of their investments in Apple. Why? "Because everything they do is so great! My wife and I use all of their products, and we love them!"

Great products. Great ads. Great customer service. This is all great stuff but not enough to make a solid investment decision. Even if Apple does well in the stock market, that doesn't mean that concentrating all your dollars into Apple will optimize your earnings or protect you if the market goes south.

Again, this makes sense as you sit here calmly. Diversification is something most of us know we should do. But when forced to make a choice, especially with too little of the right information, we default to what we know and see relationships that may not exist.

It's worth noting that people can also do the opposite and take diversification too far, spreading their investment dollars across as many vehicles and stocks as possible. This is another shortcut, based on the assumption that the more diverse your portfolio, the less risk it carries. But there's a point where diversifying doesn't reduce risk enough to be worth it.

Another shortcut is allocating dollars across your investments equally.[7] Equality is great, but when it comes to investing, this isn't necessarily the best way to go. The decision-making behind how much money you should invest and where it should go is actually quite strategic and depends on where you are in your investment journey, how long you have until retirement, and your investment goals.

Relying On Your Memory Can Lead You Astray

To understand how likely it is for something to happen in the future, you need to do some mental computing. For instance, to estimate your future investment returns, you need a lot of information, and you need to run a lot of predictive models in your head.

Can't do that?

Me neither.

Our brains can't do that kind of math (at least not without a lot of time and energy), and even then, we're often without enough data to do it correctly. So we use a substitute: our memories. Behavioral science research shows that people tend to judge the likelihood of a future event by relying on recall of past examples of a similar event.[8]

Take air travel, for example. Most of us don't think about dying each time we get on a plane. We're usually preoccupied with other thoughts, like where we're going, what we're going to do when we get there, and who we might end up sitting next to on the flight. But research has shown that if you hear about an airplane crash the day before you board a plane, you're more likely to worry about the flight. This will happen even though, statistically speaking, the chances of your plane crashing are no different than they were a week, a month, or a year ago. Even if a crash happens the day before you fly, you're still more likely to get mugged on the ground than you are to crash in the air, but our brains don't naturally rely on statistics. They do, however, rely on what they *remember*. And we can very easily remember a plane crash if we hear about it the day before a flight.

I know a few people who've made risky investment decisions because they've unknowingly fallen into this "memory trap." Not long ago, I talked to an investor who recently put the bulk of his savings into cryptocurrency, which is volatile and risky. There can be huge returns, but there's also a solid chance of substantial losses. I asked him why he made that move, given that he had previously expressed a commitment to ensure a secure future for his son. He told me about a couple of his friends who, before the most recent market downturn, saw incredible returns from their crypto investments. He figured that if they could do it, he could do it too.

This investor didn't even consider seeking out people

who regretted investing in crypto and asking them why. He didn't think about waiting to see if his friends would still be happy with their investments a few months down the road. He also didn't buy any less-risky investments to protect himself just in case. In other words, he relied on his memory and assumed that the information he already knew was all there was to know.[9] His recollection was all he needed to make his decision, and the recollection of his friends' successes was strong.

Additional Psychological Shortcuts and Biases Make Us Susceptible to Bad Investment Decisions

Unfortunately, as long as investors keep seeing growing returns from their risky decisions, they will believe they're on the right track. Even more unfortunate is the fact that if they lose money, they may likely dismiss the loss as a fluke. This is a mental bias known as *confirmation bias*[10], and it occurs when people with certain beliefs curate the information around them. They only accept the facts that support what they already believe and reject the facts that don't.

Even when presented with evidence that their investment strategy is not optimal, people under the spell of confirmation bias will likely hang firm to the notion that it is. For example, if that guy who put all his funds into Apple because he loves his iPhone was told that his decision wasn't great, he'd probably go out of his way to find evidence of Apple's strong stock performance, but he'd ignore information regarding alternative investment strategies. He might discount alternatives to the decision he already made or choose to disbelieve evidence that points to his bad decision-making. Doing this helps him justify his choice and sleep well at night.

This seems like an obvious error in judgement, one that we think we can easily avoid. But if we choose to be passive, this mental glitch happens without our being aware of it.

Sunk costs make us susceptible to another potential pitfall in investment decision-making. A sunk cost is money spent that we cannot recover.[11] When we pay for something and can't get a refund, we do what we can to get the most out of it because—and only because—we already paid for it. We do this even if "getting the most out of it" makes us miserable.

For example, we sit through a movie we can't stand because we already paid for the ticket. We force ourselves to wear uncomfortable shoes because we paid too much for them. Or we stay in relationships longer than we should, not because we feel there's hope for a better future, but because we've already put so much into it.

The way people behave with investing is no different. Many investors I've worked with are reluctant to let go of an investment vehicle or a stock simply because they've sunk so much into it already. Rather than look to the future and adjust their portfolios to optimize for wealth, they hang on to the past and lose even more. People often choose a favorite stock, usually one they think will increase in value soon, and invest heavily into it. Even once it becomes evident that the stock value won't budge, or that another option might be better, they continue to pour money into it because they've invested so heavily into it already. It's as if they don't want to give up believing until they at least get *something* out of it.

People also make bad decisions when they find themselves in a tight spot. They feel compelled to take action because they put more significance on action than on the failure to act (this is called *action bias*).[12] In other words, when faced with uncertainty, there's sometimes a human propensity to believe that doing something is better than doing nothing, whatever that something might be. On a deeper psychological level, action brings about a sense of greater control.

It's a human compulsion to fix, course correct, or frantically make things right. When I saw my stocks fall in that Wi-Fi café in Thailand, I immediately sold some of them, and it was absolutely the wrong thing to do. When stocks drop, a much better option is often to buy *more* (buy low, sell high—*not* sell low!) or to sit tight. But because I felt like I'd lost control, I felt strongly compelled to regain it. I had to *do something* to get it back, and selling was what I could do. Doing nothing would have actually been better, but I wanted to *feel* better in the moment. And doing so hurt me in the long run.

It's hard to focus on long-term thinking, and some people are biased toward immediate gratification. Research shows that people with this bias would rather be handed ten dollars today than wait one day to receive fifteen. But time is relative: the same people wouldn't care about waiting an extra day if the earliest they could get the ten dollars was a year from now. When deciding between ten bucks one year from now or fifteen bucks a year and one day from now, these folks are happy to wait an extra day to get the fifteen bucks.[13] This bias explains why some people prefer investing in ways they believe will get them immediate returns, rather than investing over the long term, being patient, and becoming more wealthy in the future. As long as there are options that yield returns in the short term, people with this bias will have the urge to take them. And they won't necessarily know they're acting on this urge.

Overconfidence bias can also be a dangerous trap, and is probably the most insidious.[14] Overconfidence creates an inability to align how much a person *truly* knows with how much they *think* they know. Or it creates confusion between how good they *really* are at something with how good they *believe* they are. Have you ever found yourself in a conversation with someone who clearly doesn't know what they're talking about, but acts like they do? Yeah, me too. If you care enough to save them from embarrassment, you might point out that they don't quite have their facts right. But when you do this to people with overconfidence bias, they often dig their heels in even more, believing in their expertise more than evidence suggests they should.

This is annoying at a party, and can be dangerous when investing.

Investing is hard, even when it seems easy. When I talk to investors with limited information and a huge amount of confidence, I worry for them, and many investors are more confident in their choices than evidence suggests they should be. Overconfident investors are more likely to engage in overtrading[15] and hang on to losing investments too long while selling winning investments too quickly.[16] All of these decisions can lead to financial outcomes that aren't great.

Investors usually don't gather as much information as they should before they invest, probably because they feel the market is too unpredictable or complex to learn. And if they're overconfident, they're even less likely to seek out evidence that might ultimately prove them wrong. Plus, given that most people seek out information from people like them, it's no wonder they go on believing that their knowledge is more accurate than it really is.

Research also suggests that overconfidence increases as the difficulty of a task increases.[17] Though it seems counter-intuitive, the harder something is to know or do, the more likely it is that people will feel confident in knowing or doing it. This phenomenon may occur because humans aren't great at assessing exactly how easy or hard a task is to begin with or how much they don't know. So, if people know a little bit about a topic or an issue, they believe they know a lot.

These are just some examples of mental shortcuts and biases that could impact your investment decisions. And as I mentioned earlier, it's not necessary to remember all of these as you make your investment choices, but it is important to be aware of these pitfalls and to know when it's time to refer to this book for guidance. (We'll offer steps you can take to circumvent these decision-making pitfalls throughout the book).

It's worth noting that not all mental shortcuts are bad. In fact, if we took no shortcuts in our decision-making, we'd struggle to move forward in many aspects of our lives. Many of our decisions are made on the spot, and many are too small to be worth thinking through diligently. But when your financial security and the financial security of your family are at stake, you want to be careful, and you need to be aware of how heuristics and biases can influence your decision-making.

To Invest Well, You Have to Be Well

We all care about our mental, emotional, and physical states of wellness. When we're sick, we try to feel better. When we're injured, we try to heal. When faced with personal struggles, we may seek therapy, talk to friends, or read self-help books. We strive to eat well, to reach or maintain a decent weight, and to sleep enough hours each night. We want to live longer and be able to do more while we're alive. Ultimately, we seek happiness, comfort, fulfillment, and a life free of injury and pain.

But what we want and what we do are two very different things. In reality, we don't always get enough sleep. We don't always eat well or exercise as much as we'd like. For many of us, our stress levels are higher than we want them to be. Some of us suffer from chronic pain, depression, or anxiety. Others of us are afflicted with obsessive-compulsive disorder, anorexia, bipolar disorder, or attention-deficit disorder, while others still may struggle with dependency on alcohol or drugs. Some of us are overcome by grief over the loss of a loved one, or regularly experience fear over the possibility of some future terrible event.

This is life, and these are common human experiences. If we lived in a perfect world, we wouldn't have to deal with these afflictions, but the world isn't perfect, so we do what we can. And we should do all we can to work through our issues and be well, because not only does wellness lead to happiness, but our states of wellness are very much related to the quality of our decision-making.

Stress, anxiety, and depression can lead to making riskier investment decisions. According to a 2017 Gallup Poll,[18] eight out of every ten Americans report experiencing stress as part of their daily lives (a little over four in ten report experiencing stress frequently). A 2018 Gallup Poll revealed that 55 percent of Americans experience stress "a lot" during the course of a day, and that people in the United States are among the most stressed globally (ranking alongside countries like Iran, Sri Lanka, and Albania).[19] According to 2017 research by the American Institute of Stress, the top causes of stress aren't rare occurrences, but the things that persist in our daily lives, like money, work, or the future of the country.[20] And these days, as people struggle to manage the social, economic, and public health implications of the COVID-19 pandemic, stress is at an all-time high.[21]

Stress has implications for our mental, emotional, and physical health, which in turn impacts decision-making in many ways. Psychologically speaking, research has revealed that stress can impair our short-term memory.[22] This makes it harder to retain information, and poor information retention means poor decisions. Some research indicates that people make riskier decisions when they are stressed. This applies to men more so than women and tends to happen more frequently after a stressful event.[23] Other research suggests that stress causes people to choose habitual options, rather than considering new choices that could be better.[24]

Stress can also have physical implications such as muscle tension, which if prolonged can lead to migraines or musculoskeletal pain.[25] Pain stemming from chronic stress can impact one's ability to process decision outcomes,[26] likely because the brain is preoccupied with processing the pain. In other words, if you're always aching, you've got less mental bandwidth to carefully think through the pros and cons of your choices.

Emotionally speaking, stress can lead one to feel overwhelmed, lonely, worthless, and in some cases suicidal.[27] These feelings are associated with depression, which is not uncommon in the United States, especially since the spread of the coronavirus. A recent Census Bureau study confirms this, with 24 percent of Americans reporting symptoms of depression.[28]

All of this matters because according to research, people with symptoms of depression are more likely to make bad decisions.[29] Depression leads to an inaccurate assessment of the pros and cons of each potential choice outcome. Specifically, depressed individuals are more likely to expect disappointment with every option in front of them, which can influence their cost-benefit analyses (and explains why it's difficult for them to get help). They're also more likely to select outcomes that have short-term benefits, which often end up harming them over the long run. If you make investment decisions while suffering from depression, you may not evaluate your options with an optimal mindset, and you might make choices that will only reap short-term returns rather than set you up for a comfortable retirement. There's no judgment here—this is simply what happens when people get depressed.

Anxiety, which in 2018 impacted 18 percent of Americans each year,[30] also has serious implications when it comes to investing. Anxiety disrupts neurons in the prefrontal cortex, the area of the brain that engages in risk-reward calculation, emotional regulation, problem-solving, and decision-making. With anxiety, both animals and humans exhibit less flexibility when it comes to adopting new strategic behaviors. They're also more likely to be distracted by irrelevant external stimuli as they make their choices: stimuli that may influence their choice but has nothing to do with their decision.[31]

Given that the act of making investment decisions alone can cause anxiety, it's no wonder many well-intentioned investment choices don't go well. Add investing to a scary economic climate, and you've got a situation tailor-made for anxiety-ridden decision-making.

Other less common disorders can also profoundly impact how people make decisions. For example, people with obsessive-compulsive or hoarding disorders are more likely to be indecisive and uncomfortable with uncertainty; both of these disorders have serious implications for one's ability to make solid decisions.[32] Those with bipolar disorder are more likely to act impulsively and feel more immune to risk.[33] People with ADHD are easily distracted as they make decisions, not just by their environment, but also by their own internal thoughts. This means they have a hard time processing possibilities, weighing options, and arriving at the right decisions. They're therefore less likely to effectively rank their options and more likely to be impulsive in their decision-making.[34]

It's not difficult to see how your emotional well-being can impact your investment choices. If you're experiencing stress, anxiety, or any other psychological challenge, your investment decisions may not be as great as you think they are. The market's inherent uncertainty can be difficult to manage, both emotionally and psychologically, especially when so much is at stake. Add this uncertainty to the stressors of everyday life, and on top of that a behavioral health condition, and you could make bad decisions without even knowing it.

This doesn't mean you're doomed. It just means you're

human. Stress might be inevitable, but leaving money on the table is not.

Poor Physical Health Can Compromise Your Investments

Your physical well-being can also have a profound impact on decision-making. Something as basic as a poor diet can lead you down the wrong decision-making path. For example, we tend to make riskier decisions when we're hungry or eating foods with low nutritional value.[35] If you skip meals, practice intermittent fasting, or start and end your day with fast food, you're probably setting yourself up to take more risks than if you had eaten well. At a minimum, try to eat regular high-nutrition meals for several days before you decide on anything investment-related. This lowers your chances of taking too many risks that could leave your portfolio vulnerable.

Lack of sleep also has serious implications for decision-making, in two major ways. First, people who are sleep-deprived are more likely to expect a reward for their risky decisions. Sleep-deprivation also causes people to be less concerned about negative consequences that arise from their risky choices.[36] This means that if you're suffering from a lack of sleep, your choices could be less safe, and you're less likely to course-correct once those choices come back to bite you. I've worked with investors who've thrown their money into risky options, seen their earnings dwindle, and yet consistently hang on to hope, firmly believing that a huge payoff will come one day, and too often it doesn't. I wonder about the sleep patterns of these investors.

Pain can also be a problem. Research has shown that chronic pain doesn't impact attention, short-term memory, or general intelligence[37], yet it still has an effect on one's decision-making capabilities. Specifically, it hinders cognitive flexibility: people with chronic pain (much like people with chronic stress) are less likely to be open to new information and more likely to engage in habitual behavior.[38] If you experience chronic pain and you're advised to consider investing in new assets, you may likely run on autopilot, sticking to what you've always done even if something new could be better.

Medical research on the relationship between wellness and decision-making is constantly progressing. The more we learn about how our states of well-being lead us down the wrong decision paths, the better equipped we can be to make investment choices that leave us feeling confident and comfortable.

You can also rely on a wealth advisor or investment planner to help you make your choices. But if you do so, make sure you know enough about your advisor's state of wellness also, or they could make poor decisions for you. As a wealth advisor, I consider it my responsibility to be as physically, emotionally, and mentally healthy as possible. I prioritize getting quality sleep. I eat well and avoid being hungry. I exercise regularly, take courses in self-improvement, and seek emotional support when I need it. The best advisors of any kind—whether in investing, personal improvement, business coaching, or another field—should prioritize their own wellness so they can make the best decisions on behalf of their clients.

If you're looking to hire a wealth advisor, interview them first and find out where they stand with their personal wellness. Let them know how your own state of wellness might influence your ability to make solid decisions. It's not easy being vulnerable and sharing what ails you, but the more your advisor knows, the more they can help. And if the advisor doesn't appreciate your vulnerability or understand why you're asking them about how they take care of themselves, then maybe they aren't the right advisor for you.

The Stories We Tell Ourselves Can Be Expensive

Many things we think are real are actually made up. I'm not saying we're delusional—I'm saying we're human. And as human beings, we create stories about the things that happen so we can make sense of them. We seem to have a need to create meaning out of events around us.[39] For example, if a lot of people frequent a particular restaurant, we might take that to mean that the food is really good.

If someone winks in our direction, we might take that to mean that they're flirting. And years ago, if there was a drought, people took that to mean that the gods needed a sacrifice.

In reality, rain has nothing to do with the gods, the number of people eating at a restaurant may have little to do with the quality of the food, and that person winking may just have something in their eye. Whatever meanings we create, the point is, *we create them*. And then we hang onto them.

Our human tendency to create meaning out of our experiences has served a valuable purpose for us. According to historian-philosopher Yuval Noah Harari, the single reason why humans have dominated all other species on the planet is our ability and propensity to create stories about how the world works, what matters and what doesn't matter, and what exists and doesn't exist.[40] Stories are unifying, allowing humans to organize in large numbers while other species are unable to do the same. Armies of thousands can rally to war around a common cause because we create stories about things worth fighting for, like freedom, human rights, or religion.

In the animal world, there's no such thing as the concept of freedom. There's no argument over rights, and there's no religion. Any rallying occurs among smaller groups, where individual animals know other animals personally. Wolf packs, for example, only grow so large because wolves are limited in how many other wolves they know well enough to trust.

People are limited in the same way, but our quest for meaning and our creation of stories allow us to do more. Shared meaning brings strangers together in a trusting bond, allowing large numbers of people to fall in love with a brand, join together in political protest, or believe and invest in something called the "stock market." Our ability to create stories that organize large groups is a super power that can be used for good or evil, and ideally, we humans strive to use it for good.

When faced with uncertainty, our craving for meaning intensifies. For example, back in middle school I had no idea how my first crush felt about me, or if she even knew who I was. So much was on the line: if she didn't like me back, my heart would be crushed. So, I looked for meaning in every little thing she did. If she smiled at me, I took that to mean she knew I existed. If she told me that she liked what I was wearing, I took that to mean she was interested. And when she handed me a note that said she wanted me to walk her home after school, I knew it was on. In the third grade, things were different. Getting kicked by a girl during recess meant she had a crush on you. The meanings of things were different, and without knowing the meaning behind each social cue, growing up can feel chaotic. Well, at least more chaotic than it already is.

Shared meaning connects us and holds our society together. It creates organization out of chaos and puts us on the same page. We might still experience social friction from time to time (which generally happens when we disagree about meaning), but life would be a lot more challenging without the meanings we share. We would find it difficult to get along, and we wouldn't know what to expect from one another.

When we need to make sense of things, we rely on meanings to fill in the gaps. This is particularly true with investing. When we invest, we often feel out of control. What we put into our portfolios today may or may not be there in five, ten, or twenty years. Regardless of what we do, the performance of our investments is largely out of our hands. New tariffs could mean an imminent dip in the stock market. An inverted yield curve could mean a recession is on its way. An expensive suit could mean your wealth advisor is going to rob you blind. And so on.

However, there is a downside to meaning-creation: once meanings are created, we tend to hang on to them quite tightly and have a hard time re-evaluating them. This can be a problem because meanings can hold us back, and the only way to improve our lives is to let go of what certain choices might mean.[41]

For example, we might want to take up motor biking at the

age of fifty because we always thought it would bring us joy. But if, according to society, doing so means we're desperately and unbecomingly clinging to our youth, then we might deprive ourselves of a little bit of happiness. In short, we might not choose the best option because doing so carries social meanings we don't want to be associated with.

Purchasing life insurance is a good example of this "meaning" in investing. Many people have embraced the story that life insurance is meant for older people with children—to protect their progeny after they pass away. Life insurance means imminent death, so you don't need to invest in it unless death is imminent. It also means that you're putting away money that can only be cashed in once you're gone. Life insurance is so connected with death that it's hard for people to uncouple the asset vehicle from the life event. And for this reason, many people who could benefit from it opt against it.

But if you look beyond its socially popular meaning, life insurance is a very smart asset protection tool for people of any age. Some life insurance policies include a component that's similar to a savings account, but with greater interest: your money grows, but that growth isn't correlated to the market. This means that even if the market tanks, the money you put into your life insurance policy won't. Moreover, if you suddenly need money in the short term to buy a home, pay for a wedding, or help a kid through college, you can borrow money from your policy at a rate so low that you'd still come out ahead. And if tragedy strikes you at an early age, your family will be covered.

Life insurance is a safety net, not a death asset. Implementing life insurance into your financial plan can provide you with the confidence to take bigger risks with other investments. If you have a life insurance policy with both death benefit and savings components, your cash value can grow slowly and steadily, and generally upward.

This doesn't mean life insurance is the only financial planning vehicle one should use, but it's something that anyone striving for a diversified plan should seriously consider. Still, many investors reject the idea of life insurance because of what it means, not because of what it really is.

Many investors also believe the story that hiring a money manager or investment or wealth advisor means they're throwing money away, because money managers and advisors are swindlers who get rich from the fees they charge. But this isn't always true, and trading on your own online also involves fees. Whether or not a wealth advisor is actually useful depends on your situation and your goals, and whether or not the advisor is only out for themself depends on the individual advisor. In many circumstances, and for many people, it's quite valuable to hire someone to constantly keep an eye on their portfolio and adjust it to maximize returns. They might pay a fee to the advisor, but they also might make a lot more money than if they had done it themselves. Even if you prefer to trade online yourself, it may be worth hiring someone to manage aspects of your portfolio while you dabble in the market.

When You Align Your Choices with How You See Yourself (or How Others Might See You), Bad Decisions Can Happen

Many people trade stocks themselves because doing so means they are empowered and self-sufficient. I've talked with some do-it-yourself investors who believe trading without a money manager means they're savvy and well-positioned to beat the system. They've created meaning around who they are as people from their do-it-yourself approach. This is a unique type of meaning-creation: the creation of individual identity.[42] Our personal identities emerge when the meanings we create aren't about the world but about ourselves, who we are, and what we stand for.

Our identities can be important and powerful. They help us define who we are. They give us a sense of belonging, connecting us to a larger group of people who share our interests, values, or beliefs. And many political movements that have shaped our society and culture (like movements for race or gender equality) have been based on identity.[43] Whether you identify as a Christian, a woman, a runner, an engineer, a homosexual, a birdwatcher, or a bad-ass investor, your identity can empower you, support you, and make you feel you are part of something big and meaningful.

But like meaning-creation in general, there's a dark side to identity: hanging onto an identity can hurt us in certain situations, especially if we don't challenge it. Imagine a high school senior who is accepted into Harvard concluding she's highly intelligent and therefore special, when it could be that she owes her accomplishment largely to her stable upper-class home life. But because acceptance into Harvard has come to mean you're uniquely intelligent, this is what she believes. If she lives by this identity, many of her subsequent life decisions could be influenced by it in ways that could hurt her. She may limit her friendships to people who attend Ivy League schools and deprive herself of interactions with people who aren't college-educated but could enrich her life. She may pursue a career befitting someone "like her," even if it may not be what makes her happy. And she may decide against some very smart investments because they're not what "someone smart like her" would choose.

When people make identity-based decisions, they fail to prioritize options that might be better for them.[44] For example, some people might choose to purchase over-priced running shoes from a popular brand because the brand speaks to their identity as a driven athlete. Never mind the shoes may not be worth the price tag: it's not the shoe that's being paid for, it's the personal identity that the brand speaks to. These types of decisions aren't necessarily bad, but they're likely to be less than optimal if we make choices based on identity and not the actual benefit we expect to gain.

When identity-driven purchasing is applied to investing, people can end up buying stock based on who they are and want to be rather than on what works best for their portfolio. This kind of identity-driven decision-making can be problematic, given that the goal of investing is financial security, not feeling better about the kind of person you are.

Others can also assign us identities or "labels" that are limiting, and we can assign identities that limit others.[45] For example, if your high school-aged son sleeps in regularly, you might conclude that he's lazy, when perhaps he's physically unwell or depressed. If your neighbor doesn't wave hello when you wave to them, you might conclude that they're rude when maybe they're just shy. If someone corrects your grammar on social media, you may decide they're pompous when really, they might just care and want to help you avoid embarrassment.

People raised in abusive homes experience labelling in a particularly harmful way. Abusive parenting confuses children, so they create self-identities to make sense of it all. These kids grow up embracing the identity of someone who is "no good" or "a worthless loser," and they carry these meanings all the way through adulthood. Sometimes parents explicitly label their children in these negative ways. Then, these children grow up and make decisions in their adult lives based on flawed identities. They may tolerate an abusive spouse, take a job that's beneath them, or accept mistreatment from social institutions. They may also decide to not bother with investing because they severely under-value their own lives and future.

Generally speaking, we dislike bad labels and prefer good ones. We want others to see us as smart, successful, and likeable. When we are successful with our investments, we like the idea that others might see us as financially intelligent. If we make huge returns one year, sell our stocks, and buy a huge home, we like how this home might make us look to our friends and acquaintances. We want to come across as successful, and we want others to see us that way. I know I did, before I lost it all.

When our identities cause us trouble, we may need to come to terms with our egos. *Ego* is a powerful thing, and quite sneaky. Eckhart Tolle describes ego as a dark side of self-identity.[46] According to Tolle, ego is a shell that separates you from others, that creates disconnection, and is based on narratives that are not necessarily true but are accepted as true. Tolle writes about ego as if it has a mind of its own and is always under threat. Because the ego is constantly protecting its existence, it rejects ideas and actions that challenge it. If the ego is insanely huge, it will do what it can to stay huge. You know that person who has to be the center of attention? The decisions they make are likely all about remaining the center of attention, even if those decisions are bad.

People tied up in protecting their egos and identities are less likely to make investment choices that can protect them. For example, they might focus on huge real estate investments they can't really afford because others can't see their stocks, but they can see their huge new property. This ego-protection strategy can leave people financially vulnerable.

It's not a great idea to buy a ton of real estate just because doing so makes us feel special. It's much better to diversify our portfolios and be more secure. It's not wise to go after hot or trendy investments because we want to feel smart. It's much better to actually *be* smart and go after the right investments.

These are just some of the ways in which meaning and identity-creation impact our investment decisions and keep us from having the right mindset. You'll learn more about how this plays out in actual investment decisions in future chapters.

When Your Decisions Follow Social Norms and Expectations More Than the Numbers, You Might End Up Worse Off

Norms are social rules that a group of people share, rules that maintain order and cohesion.[47] In fact, if the stories we create about the world around us (our meaning-creation) are perpetuated long enough and become reinforced, they can drive the creation of norms.

For example, years ago, when most people embraced the idea that being homosexual meant you were psychologically ill, homosexuals experienced seriously negative social and legal consequences. As the meaning of "being homosexual" changed over time, so did our norms and our laws.[48]

Some norms are formal rules, also known as laws and regulations, and there are legal consequences for not following them. The norm of stopping at a red light or not committing murder are examples. Other norms are informal; they aren't written in a code or law book anywhere, but they're followed by most people nonetheless. There's nothing illegal about wearing flippers, a mask, and a snorkel on an airplane, but it's just not the norm.

We learn norms through the process of socialization. As we grow up, our parents, teachers, and institutions train us on how to behave (what we ought and ought not to do). We also learn new norms when we experience dramatic social change. The norm of social distancing emerged with

COVID-19, and it didn't take long for (most) people to learn what behavior was acceptable and what wasn't. In these types of situations, norms can spread like a virus.

Some norms are great: they keep us alive and sane, and they keep society running smoothly. Norms are meant to keep us all on the same page, and when we're on the same page, we experience life as predictable and reliable. This is important to us. The less predictable the events around us feel, and the less sure we are about the behavior of others, the more likely things can start to unravel. Imagine driving each day and approaching intersections with no idea if other drivers were going to stop or drive right through. You'd white-knuckle every drive, even just going two miles down the road to the grocery store.

But sometimes the norm isn't best for us. At one point, smoking was the norm. Slavery was the norm. Sometimes norms need to be questioned, challenged, and changed. Sometimes norm disruption makes things better, even when changes to the status quo are uncomfortable.

When it comes to investing, people follow norms all the time, when a lot of those norms might not be best. It's the norm to invest in your company's 401K if they have one, but is this always the best decision? If your company isn't matching your contributions, or if the match is quite low, you might be better off investing that money elsewhere.

It's considered the norm for people to strive for home own-ership, largely because homes are understood to appreciate in value. But for some people, and in some circumstances, home ownership is not a financially sound decision. For some, investing in another asset makes more sense. It's also the norm to put off getting life insurance until you're older and have children, but does following this norm put you in the best financial position? Not necessarily.

It's important to be aware of the norms that may be shaping your decisions, and it's important to question them. Some normative investment behavior needs to be critically chal-lenged, or you could walk right into an investment plan that leaves you vulnerable. The right investment mindset involves being mindful of the decisions you *don't* make as much as the decisions you do make.

Cultural Expectations Can Override Rational Decision-Making and Lead to Sub-Par Investment Decisions

There are so many definitions of culture out there, but for the purposes of this book, we'll define culture as "the institutionalization of a society's customs and values."[49] When a set of customs or values of a society are practiced regularly and widely shared to where even people *outside* of the society can recognize them, we can say they're institu-tionalized, and a culture exists. The types of food people in a society regularly eat is part of their culture. How people dress is cultural, as is their language. And how a society goes about traditions, like getting married, looks very different from one culture to another.

Culture shapes decision-making. It's a mistake to assume that decisions stem solely from our personal attributes or efforts (there's a term for this: *fundamental attribution error*).[50] We don't live in a vacuum. Our cultural context influences our decision-making in multiple ways. Scholars of decision-making recognize that people consciously or unconsciously consider the impact of their decisions on a number of different levels, from how accountable they'll be for their decision, to who is affected by it, to how familiar the various elements of the decision are to them.[51] Culture shapes all of these things. According to some perspectives, culture influences mental schemas, rules, and goals in ways that shape the options we think we have and how valuable the trade-offs to each of our options are. Culture also impacts how successfully we can gather and interpret all the information we need.[52]

We see the impact of culture in decision-making every day. Consider the research suggesting that, when faced with competitive pressure, firms led by CEOs who are second or third generation immigrants experience higher profitability than the average company.[53] Research by marketing scholars indicates that culture influences consumer financial decision-making, so much so that experts recommend marketers of financial services firms take culture into account when managing customers.[54]

Research reported in the *Harvard Business Review* indicates that businesses in different cultures handle decision-making differently. In the United States, India, Italy, Mexico, and Russia, final decision-making is usually the task of one person: the boss. Decisions are made quickly but are flexible and subject to change. Decision-makers in these cultures regularly pivot under new conditions or with new information. In Germany, Japan, the Netherlands, and Sweden, the decision-making process is more time-consuming and painstaking, as everyone strives for consensus and spends time gathering as much information as possible. But once the choice is made, it's implemented quickly and not easily changed. Everyone is aligned on what needs to be done.

Interesting, and also a little "meta," is research indicating that whether or not someone believes in the influence of culture is driven by the culture itself. For example, Americans are more likely to say that individuals are solely responsible for their decisions, whereas the Chinese are more likely to recognize the role that society and culture play in decision-making.[55]

Culture plays a part in investing, as well. Talk to investors in Singapore, and you'll learn they have a different perspective than Americans on which investment vehicles are ideal. While investing in the stock market is the norm in the United States, investors in Singapore generally consider stock market investments to be pure gambling. In Singapore, life insurance and real estate are king. Stocks aren't something you automatically invest in; you dabble in them with extra money you have if you want to play the odds and take your chances, like going to Vegas. It's very likely that these differences in investment decision-making reflect Singapore's generally more risk-averse culture versus countries like the United States.[56]

Research from the University of Zurich describes other ways in which culture influences financial decision-making.[57] Even after controlling for inflation and accumulated wealth, researchers discovered that investors in Eastern Europe are highly risk-averse, while investors in the United States are described as "ego-traders" on the hunt for quick gains. In Africa, investors are even more impatient than American traders, culturally inclined to prefer smaller returns in the immediate future than to wait for larger returns. Nordic traders are on the other end of the spectrum—they're much more patient in seeing returns.

Another interesting finding from this study is that wealthier investors are more likely to pay attention to their policy statements, whereas those with smaller portfolios invest more by emotion. This suggests the possibility of subcultural influences on investment decisions as well. It could be a mistake to assume that each country has a homogenous culture that influences all of its residents in the same way. For example, people raised in Manhattan are likely to make decisions differently than those raised in a rural town in the deep South. Different areas of the United States have different "cultures."[58]

We even see different subcultures emerge within a single city. In the Seattle area, where I live, a burgeoning tech culture has emerged, replete with its own style of clothing, food and beverage preferences, and language. If you're not working with or for a tech company, you may not understand why so many tech folks look, talk, and behave the way they do. Many of my clients work in the technology space, but I also have friends who work in the service industry or in construction. If you look closely at how they dress, what they do for fun, and the way they communicate, you can see they're all different.

Ultimately, the point is to recognize that although our norms and culture influence us to make decisions in particular ways, this isn't to say that those ways are best for us when it comes to choosing investments. The right investment mindset is about questioning if and how much your decisions are best for you, and how much your culture (or subculture) influences your decisions.

Be Honest, Not Perfect, Because Perfection is a Pipe Dream

There are many ways in which individual and social influences shape our investment decision-making, and we've covered the most relevant. Insights regarding human decision-making continue to grow as new research is conducted, and new research is conducted all the time. Staying on top of the information can become a bit daunting, but you don't need to do everything correctly to become a more confident investor.

The right mindset isn't about being perfect. It's about being radically honest about the fact that we don't arrive at many of our decisions thoughtfully, rationally, or free of irrelevant influence. It's about being aware that no matter how smart we are and how hard we try, we're too human to be totally rational. It's about accepting the reality that, left to our natural devices, our choices are likely to be sub-optimal, even when everything on the surface seems to be OK.

Sometimes bad decisions still result in great outcomes. You might be reckless in making an investment decision but reap massive rewards. This doesn't necessarily mean your decision was good, or that you had the right mindset. Maybe you just got lucky, and maybe that luck won't happen again. When it comes to investing, you can't rely on luck. The right mindset is aware that luck is random. The right mindset is also aware that even the best-made decisions could be followed by huge losses, because the market is unpredictable.

This is why the right mindset isn't about making tons of money. It's about increasing your chances of being financially protected, while simultaneously increasing your chances of making financial gains. It's about preparing for as many possibilities as you can, and doing so rationally, carefully, thoughtfully, and strategically.

In the chapters that follow, I'll explain how to move from awareness to action. I'll show you how to increase your chances of success by following a set of rules designed to protect you from decision-making flaws.

CHAPTER 3

THE MINDSET RESET

When making investment decisions, a lot can go wrong. It's as though every way you turn, something other than rationality drives your choices. And maybe that's OK; sometimes we don't want to make rational decisions. Sometimes we choose an option not because it's the best one, but because we want to feel better in the short term. Or we might make a decision that's bad for us as individuals but that will nurture our connections with others. This is all OK as long as we're on top of it, and as long as it's not manipulating us.

When it comes to investing, some goals override all others. For example, it's more important to use your investments to maximize earnings than to become socially popular. When our choices don't lead us to the goals we need to achieve, we owe it to ourselves to find a better way.

And there's always a better way.

There are specific practices every investor can follow to optimize their decision-making and set themselves up for success. Nika and I have identified five mindset practices that can lead to more confident investing and a better life.

First, When Making a Decision, Ask Yourself, "What Influences Are at Play Here?" In Other Words, Be Aware!

Awareness is important. It sounds like a small thing, but just knowing that human decision-making is subject to internal and external influences—from how you sleep to who your close friends are—is a huge step. The reason why we humans experience most of the problems we do is because we don't see them coming. By assuming that your decision-making isn't rational means you're already engaging in radical open-mindedness, allowing you to see possibilities that weren't evident before.

Every time you face an investment decision (or any major decision), ask yourself this important question: "What influences other than rationality are at play here?" Asking this question begs for answers, which can lead you down an information-gathering path to get you to a better place. You can refer to the previous chapter to determine what might be influencing you, mentally, emotionally, physically, socially, and culturally.

Second, Ask Yourself If You're Sleeping Well, Eating Well, and Getting Your Overall Personal Wellness In Order—If Not, Assume Your Decisions Are Risky, and Adjust Accordingly

In an ideal world, you'd be getting enough sleep. Your diet would have the right amount of macro- and micro-nutrients, and you'd never be hungry. You'd never feel pain or suffer from a behavioral disorder. And stress? Forget about it. In a perfect world, there would be no stress.

But we live in the real world, and in this world we can't avoid what often ails us. Which is why the right investment mindset involves accepting that we're going to make imperfect decisions because we're not able to be perfectly well.

If you lack sleep, don't eat well, have OCD, etc., don't assume you can push through and make good choices despite it all. The human body isn't good at that. Instead, assume that you're likely to be more impulsive, biased toward the habitual, or likely to over-favor short-term rewards. Then, as you make your decisions, you can correct for what you know might be your flaws. For example, if you know that a poor state of wellness can make you impulsive, then err on the side of over-thinking your important decisions. Chances are your version of "over-thinking" won't be over-thinking at all.

It's like driving a car that's out of alignment. If your car keeps veering to the left, and you can't take it to get serviced, you need to drive by pulling the steering wheel to the right. It's the only way you can make sure not to drive off the road.

Third, Ask "Why?" about Everything (Especially Decisions or Beliefs You Typically Take for Granted) and then Ask, "Why Not an Alternative?"

A lot of normative investment tactics or behaviors make a ton of sense, or they wouldn't be the norm. Cultures and sub-cultures favor certain investment options for a reason. But sometimes the norm, or what's culturally accepted, isn't best for you. Just because everyone at the tailgate party is drinking heavily doesn't mean the one diabetic in attendance should also be drinking.

It's the norm for people to invest in their company's 401K. I've talked to many people who tell me they've been "investing for a while." They come across as experienced, seasoned investors, so I automatically wonder about their stock portfolio and I'm curious if they're investing in bonds, have an annuity account, have a life insurance policy, or own investment property. But when I ask for details, I'm often surprised when they tell me they're contributing to their company's 401K, and that's it.

The 401K is unique because it's the only investment vehicle that falls into our laps. By the simple virtue of being employed, many of us are introduced to it and given the impression that it's *the* way to plan for retirement, but we don't experience any other investment vehicles this way. No other investments are as "normal" as the 401K, so a lot of people embrace it and throw everything they can into it without thinking twice. Investing in a 401K is such standard behavior that many people think it's the sum total investment they need for retirement.

But investing in your company's 401K isn't always a good idea. It's the norm, but that doesn't mean it's *ideal*. In fact, there are a lot of crappy 401K plans out there that aren't worth investing in. Some companies don't contribute, offer a very small match, or offer a plan with high fees. If you have one of these plans, you might be better off foregoing any 401K contributions and putting that money toward a better overall investment strategy. If you don't ask, "Why should I invest in this 401K?" you may never get the information you need to decide if your company's particular plan is worth it.

Asking "why" may seem obvious, but you'd be surprised at how often I recommend a specific investment strategy to someone who accepts it or rejects it (in total or in part) without asking me why I've selected the options I have for them, which I always select for very good reasons. For instance, I include life insurance in many of my financial plans. Some people say "yes," and some say "no." But too many base their decisions on what they already know about life insurance and what they believe it means. Most think it's not the norm until you are older and have kids, and by thinking about it you accept your mortality.

Fewer people ask, "Why life insurance?" than they should. And because they don't ask why, they don't *learn* why, which means they can't verify whether or not their decision to do "what's always been done" is really best for them. Referring back to our earlier analogy: they don't know if they're the one diabetic getting drunk at the party.

Ask "why" and ask it always, for every single important option you have, even when you think you know the answer. Let me repeat the most important part: *even when you think you know the answer.* You can ask "why" of your investment planner, your smart friend with investing experience, or yourself. Just be sure to ask.

And don't just ask why a particular vehicle or stock is worthy of investing in. Ask why it exists in the first place, and what function it's meant to serve. These questions are important. They enable you to gather the right information to make the right decisions.

Another important question to ask that can prevent norms or culture from swaying your decisions is: "Why not the alternatives?" It's not enough to know about the benefits of each investment tool—you also need to know how each tool may or may not be better than others. Stocks can do things for you that bonds can't, and vice versa. Life insurance can benefit you under circumstances that annuities weren't meant to address. Compare and contrast alternatives, but don't do it based on general knowledge about what they're normally used for. Rather, evaluate them based on hard evidence about their purpose and benefits. Be aware that policies and regulations regarding investment vehicles may change, so what you learn today may not apply in a year or two. Don't rely on old information. Keep asking.

It's also worth thinking about the norm of retirement itself and questioning whether or not you should retire in the way that's expected in our culture. In the United States, the social norm is for retirement to occur at a particular age, usually sixty-five, in part to make room in the workforce for younger workers. After retirement, American adults are no longer expected to fulfill typical social obligations like working or contributing to society, but still benefit from financial support. They can care for themselves, are free to do as they please, and enjoy the last years of their lives. This is what investors largely save for: to support their basic needs when they stop working. They also invest to fund hobbies, travel, or other experiences.

Retiring at sixty-five is so taken for granted that most people (and many investment planners) will design retirement plans without even considering the option of retiring earlier. It's also taken for granted that retirement means a person will no longer work, but this shouldn't be an automatic expectation, even if it's the cultural norm.

Other cultures have different norms when it comes to retirement. For example, in Fulani, West Africa, retirement occurs when a couple marries off their last child, at which point they're considered "socially dead," dependents of their eldest son, and deprived of all but marginal social rights. In the Andes, "retirement" doesn't mark the end of work but rather a transition to less demanding forms of work. The elderly in their culture are still expected to make a contribution to society, but they only do what they're capable of doing at their age. In Burma, the elderly transition out of economic work, but they still "work" in other ways, such as volunteering in religious organizations and engaging more heavily in religious ceremonies and observances. Their families support them financially while they do good deeds.[59]

If we were to stop and ask about alternatives to the expected American retirement, we could open ourselves up to experiences in our later years that aren't typical, usual, or normative, but more fulfilling to us as individuals. In our culture, it's expected that only those born very rich, or those lucky enough to strike it rich at a young age, are able to retire early. But if you play your investment plan right, you might be able to retire earlier than the norm. And if you don't get that chance, you may be able to set up your investments so your children can. It's also possible to formally retire at sixty-five but to continue to work at a lesser capacity. For example, one man Nika interviewed while writing this book retired after decades of experience as a mechanical engineer, but he was invited back by his company to work flexible, part time, post-retirement hours as a consultant and mentor. There are options beyond the norm for retirement.

To find these alternatives to the "norm," you need only question the origin and purpose of each option in front of you. Some choices might feel thoughtful, but they could be automatically chosen by you because "it's just how things are done." Unless you stop and examine the reasons for each of your investment choices and make sure each one lines up with your goals, you might be acting on autopilot and investing in a sub-optimal way.

Fourth, As You Narrow Down Your Different Choices, Ask Yourself What Choosing Each Option Means *to* You and *about* You

I've found that different investment vehicles mean different things to different people, and these meanings are what they use to make investment decisions. For instance, people have told me annuities are for those who aren't good at managing their own money in retirement, investing in cryptocurrency means you're on top of what's hot and trending, and stock market investing is straight-up gambling.

Sometimes the meanings we create around investment vehicles are based in truth, but many times they aren't. Sometimes the meanings that were true in the past are now outdated. Annuities have changed a lot over the years and aren't just for people who are bad at managing money. Investing in something that's trending doesn't mean it's the right investment decision. And stock market investing, if done right, is not the same as playing a slot machine.

Sometimes people will invest in a company just because it's a cool brand. Others invest in a company because they love how innovative that company is. I've seen people buy stock in a company because they identify with the company's tagline, slogan, or mission. Brands mean things to people, and that's what brands want. It's how they make money: they relate to consumers on an emotional level, and connect with consumers through a shared identity. But investing because you love a brand may not be the right way to go.

To keep your decisions from falling under the negative influences of meaning-making, ask yourself what each option means to you. Take Pete, for example. Pete is in the market for a car, and as he's shopping, he finds himself more attracted to the fast, impractical, gas-guzzling sports car than the economical sedan that he's also considering. He could dive into the decision to buy the sports car, but he feels strongly that he might regret it. It's way out of his price range, and it's a two-seater, which doesn't make sense given that he's a father of two. By all accounts, the sports car isn't the smart decision.

But he's very close to buying it anyway.

Pete might stop himself and ask, "Should I buy this sports car, or should I buy the sedan?" This is how we usually frame our decisions, in terms of this or that, yes or no. This type of question framing typically leads to a seemingly rational analysis of each option (the sedan is more efficient and affordable; the sports car is more fun, etc.). But research has shown that emotions are a huge driver of purchase decision-making when it comes to cars, so weighing pros and cons usually goes out the window.[60] Pete is trying to be rational, but it may not matter in the end.

However, Pete could also ask himself, "What does my attraction to this sports car *mean*?" It could mean Pete is superficial and values appearance. It could mean (in his own mind) he will finally be successful in life, because in his social group (and in our society), a car like this one equates to wealth and success. Or, it could mean Pete has reached a point in his life where he's sick and tired of following the rules and going by the book. Maybe, for once, Pete would like to do something impulsive and crazy.

None of these answers get Pete any closer to understanding why he likes the sports car better. But it does get him closer to understanding why he's about to abandon all reason and buy a car he'll regret buying.

Let's assume Pete's answer is that he's tired of doing things by the book. He can then take this one step further and ask what *that* means. In other words, what does the fact that he's tired of predictability mean *to him and to others*? Why does it matter to him to abandon predictability now? Let's assume Pete's answer is the following: "I've lived my whole life by the book, and it got me nowhere. My wife just divorced me, I only get to see my kids on the weekends, and I lost my house, so maybe it's time to try a different approach."

Pete can take this even further and ask what *that answer* means. Or he can stop and realize that the real question isn't whether or not he should buy the car, but whether or not he was wrong to have lived his life "by the book." If he digs deeper, maybe he'd discover it means he's been living his life according to *other people's* standards. He may then be open to living a more fulfilling and free-spirited life without sinking money he doesn't have into an impractical sports car. In other words, he can find ways to fulfill his need for spiritual freedom without compromising his wallet by buying an expensive car.

The same technique of questioning can be used when making investment decisions. For example, Milo wants to invest in real estate, and only real estate. He believes that real estate will always appreciate in value, making it a sure thing. He owns four investment properties in addition to his own home, and when he's ready to retire, he plans to sell his properties and live off the money he makes.

I've told investors like Milo that this is a very risky strategy. Real estate does generally appreciate over time, but the value of real estate can drop, and it has dropped dramatically in recent history. Even though it's also recovered, the timing of that drop and recovery is what really counts. If Milo's property loses substantial value right at the moment he wants to sell and retire, he may not have as much as he needs to retire comfortably. Or if he retires during a recession or a slump when people aren't buying real estate, he could be in trouble.

Also, if something happens in Milo's life before retirement that requires him to liquidate funds right away, he may find himself in a tough spot. Depending on the quality of the property, the timing, and the state of the economy when he needs the money, his homes could sell within a month, or it could take as long as a year. If he needs emergency funds, he might struggle. Diversifying across stocks, bonds, real estate, and other vehicles would better protect Milo. And with other investment tools, if he needed money right away, he could get it. But Milo is not convinced.

Milo could benefit from asking himself the question: "What does owning real estate mean to me?" Milo might consider that to him, real estate means security. Real estate is tangible. When you purchase it, you can see it, feel it, and experience the benefits right away. You can get renters and see their rent checks come in every month. Milo feels he can count on real estate because it's real, whereas stock earnings are elusive.

But then, Milo might ask, "What does owning *only* real estate mean to me?" In other words, instead of owning four properties, why not just own two and put the rest of his money into other vehicles, especially ones that are more resilient to change in the real estate market? Why not cover himself? Milo thinks on this and realizes that for him, property ownership means status. He recalls instances in his childhood when his parents told him that home ownership means you've pulled yourself out of the lower class, and *multiple* home ownership means you're a member of the upper class. Never mind that this isn't necessarily true; there are many multiple homeowners and property managers who struggle to make ends meet, and many wealthy people with only one home. But for Milo, the actual dollars (his earnings) don't count. The *meaning* of home ownership is what counts. That's what he's paying for and betting his future on.

This leads to the second way of making sure that meaning-making isn't problematically driving your decisions: ask what each possible decision means about *who you are*. By doing so, you'll see how each decision resonates with your *personal identity*.

Try filling the blanks in this statement: "If I (decide to) ___ then I would be (a) ___." Milo might say, "If I own a lot of real estate, then I would be a person of high status. I'd be someone important or special." It's not particularly wise to choose your investments based on how much they'll perpetuate your identity as a high-status person. This is what happens when ego takes over and makes your decisions for you. It can leave you vulnerable. If Milo truly wants to be a person of high status and wealth, then he might want to invest in a way that will *actually* increase wealth. He'd diversify, cover all bases, and prepare for all contingencies.

Lila is another investor who feels she's finally making enough income to dabble in the stock market. She decides right away that she only wants to invest in tech stocks. Before pulling the trigger, she might do well to slow down for a moment and ask, "What does it *mean* to invest *only* in technology stocks?" She's heard about the value of diversifying her portfolio, but she isn't doing that. She realizes she prefers technology stocks because "technology" to her is synonymous with "strong returns." But when she thinks more carefully, she realizes other types of stocks are also associated with strong returns.

She asks again, "What does it *mean* to only invest in technology stocks? Not just in general, but also about *who I am*?" She realizes that for her, investing in technology means investing in the future. It means supporting the progress of the human race, and more than that, she likes to think of herself as someone who is technologically progressive. It makes her feel cool. But is this the right reason to invest in a particular stock?

The best reason for Lila (or anyone) to choose any investment vehicle or stock is if doing so helps increase the likelihood of financial security for the future. If she wants to support technological progress, she can donate her volunteer time to a technology company, or she can work in the tech field and be directly involved in what she believes is progress. Meanwhile, she can create a diversified portfolio that is designed to maximize her retirement income so she can cover her bases when she's too old to work. But unless she dives into the meanings behind her choices, she can't know if her choices line up with the goals that matter. And she might retire with less money than she should.

To be sure meaning-making and identity-creation (a.k.a.

your ego) aren't driving you down the wrong decision path, look for meaning in every decision you make. Note that by "look for meaning," we don't mean to look for pros and cons, or consequences. We mean to look for meanings that are shared across society—the ones we internalize as part of our identities. Look for meanings like, "property means wealth" (which it doesn't necessarily), or "investing in technology means doing good for humanity" (which may not be accurate or the best rationale). Once you become skilled at identifying the meanings behind your options, you can prevent from being swayed by them suboptimally.

Fifth, Ask Yourself How You Might Prove What You "Know," and How Someone Who Disagrees with You Might Prove You Wrong

Our minds are complex, but the world is complicated— much more complicated than the human brain has the ability to process. This is why people rely on mental shortcuts as they make decisions. It's much too difficult to analyze every single possible alternative, and besides, who has the time?

The problem occurs when we take shortcuts without being aware that we're doing it. This is a very human and common phenomenon. If we're short on time when we make our decisions (e.g., late for work), we aren't making a high-stakes decision (type of coffee beverage to order at Starbucks), we feel the options in front of us are pretty similar (cappuccino, latte, macchiato), and we're pretty much OK with whatever happens (just need caffeine), then mental shortcuts are real time and energy savers.

Most of the decisions we make are like these, and shortcuts can often help more than they hurt. Besides, if you don't love the salad you ordered at lunch, no big deal. If you don't like the movie you rented, it's really OK. If the jeans you bought look way less flattering on you at home than they did at the store, then you can just take them back. If you make any of these types of decisions using heuristics or even relying on your biases, then there's no major harm done (unless your biases involve avoiding a business because of the race, gender, or sexual orientations of its employees, but that's a topic for a different conversation).

When our human minds play tricks on us, they do so to make life easier. But if you're putting a chunk of your monthly income into investments and relying on those investments to support you in retirement, then you may not want mental shortcuts or biases to sway your decision-making. This means you need to catch those heuristics and biases in the act before they lead to a bad decision.

One of the most sinister of all biases is overconfidence. Overconfidence can be problematic because it inherently leads one to believe there's no reason to worry about making a bad decision. There's no need to be aware, reflective, or open to what could go wrong. Overconfidence tells us everything we're doing is perfectly OK, even when it's not.

To avoid overconfidence, try asking this question: "How do I know what I claim to know?" or "How do I know this decision or action is the right one?" In other words, before acting, slow down and set out to prove your point of view to your worst critic, or as if you have to present your case in a court of law.

This question is important because it doesn't tackle the actual decision, but rather the information that drives it. Every good decision must rely on solid intel, reliable data, and relevant evidence. Yet too often, we feel certain we know something but have no real idea how we know it. I do this, too.

For instance, many entrepreneurs "know" they have a great business idea before they launch their business. They just *know* what they want to sell is something people really want to buy. But how do they know this? They often rely on their gut or personal experience, but their gut can be misleading (bias) and their experiences are limited (heuristics). Typically speaking, without market validation there's no way for them to know whether or not they have a solid business idea. Unfortunately, too few entrepreneurs spend the time and money up front to validate their concept, and their business ends up struggling.

The same can be said for authors of books. They "know" they're writing something people want to read, but how do they know this when only people in their close circle of friends have read their manuscript? Unless their books sell, they can't know for sure. They need evidence.

Not knowing how we know something doesn't mean our knowledge isn't accurate; it just means it's not validated. And we need to validate it. Without validation and evidentiary support, it's easy to be overconfident. And when you're overconfident, you won't even consider that you may be susceptible to mental shortcuts or biases. You won't open yourself up to becoming aware. But when you back up your assertions with hard facts, and those hard facts don't exist like you thought they did, your confidence is less sustainable.

It takes a huge amount of ego-checking to do this work. But again, when your finances and retirement are at stake, you can't let your ego get in the way. Your ego won't buy you groceries when you're seventy-five and no longer have an income.

As you ask yourself, "How do I know what I know?" make sure you're relying on evidence that's *objective and based on enough data points*. By objective, I mean that you aren't relying on investment information from one biased source. A seller of annuities is inclined to tell you how great annuities are. A seller of life insurance is inclined to tell you how great life insurance is, and a real estate agent is inclined to tell you how great investing in real estate is. Each of them may be right, but as you listen to them, just know they may each have a unique and limited perspective. So listen to *all* of them.

As you do so—and this is important—don't listen to their *advice*. Instead, listen to their *information*. Take in the objective information and weed out their opinions. This also applies when reading blogs or books, or watching experts on television. Weed out facts from opinion, then use those facts to determine if your own opinion is objectively supported.

How can you tell the difference? You ask *"Why?"*

If someone can't back up their statements with evidence, or with fact-based information or data, then they are giving you their opinion, which could be biased. Look for evidence like you would if you needed to prove a case in front of a judge.

Once you've proven your own point of view, set out to prove yourself wrong. For every position you firmly believe in, take on the role of an opponent whose only goal in life is to show you just how wrong you are. Sounds odd, as though you're making things hard for yourself, but you're actually making yourself more confident by doing this. For example, if you firmly believe that a 401K plan is all you need, then pretend that you are your worst enemy who wants to prove that a 401K plan alone is insufficient. What evidence would that person need to prove they're right? Seek out that evidence. If it doesn't exist, or if it's weak, then you can be more confident in your knowledge. But if you investigate and find that a 401K plan alone isn't enough, then you may have to rethink what you "know."

We're likely to look for similarities between things, like two companies we want to invest in, or two advisors we've worked with. But the human brain has a tendency to focus only on what's in front of it. When seeking out evidence of what you know, be on the lookout for what you don't know, and be aware of connections you're making that are based on incomplete information.

For example, Paula is looking to buy her second investment property. She did well with her first property she bought five years ago and recently sold it for a hefty profit. This time around, she's looking for a home that's very similar to the one she just sold: same size, same kind of neighborhood, similar features. She's convinced that what worked last time will work again.

She finds a home that meets her criteria and she buys it. But its value doesn't increase in the way she expected. She failed to realize that in her effort to find ways in which the properties were similar, she didn't look closely enough at how they were different. Her first property was located near an up-and-coming trendy part of town near shops, restaurants, and entertainment. The second property is also located near shops and restaurants, but the crime rate in the area is higher, and the schools aren't great. If we only pay attention to what's at top of mind, we could miss something important.

Also, try not to rely on just a small number of examples when you draw general conclusions (this is known as *the law of small numbers*).[61] For example, if I perform above average at my job as a wealth advisor for three years in a row, I might conclude that I'm an excellent advisor. This might be true, but three is a small number, and three years' worth of job performance isn't enough to conclude much. As it happens, I have performed well above average at my company for the past couple of years, and there is data to support this. But all this data shows is that I performed above average for the past couple of years, not that I am in fact a superior wealth advisor. To know whether or not I'm actually better than others in my field, I need to compare my performance to that of all existing wealth advisors on a number of different metrics, over a number of years. And if I really wanted to be rigorous in my analysis, I'd control for factors like region of the country, number of years advising, and other variables that might influence the number and wealth of clients an advisor like me might have.

Unfortunately, many situations don't allow for the gathering of mounds of data. This is why we use shortcuts. However, *knowing* that you don't have enough data points to draw a general conclusion is much better than *assuming* you do. Being aware of the law of small numbers can save you from being overly confident about your conclusions. If one of your stocks performed better than average over the past three to four years, it may not be wise to throw all your money into that stock. You might still make great returns from it, but all you really know is that it's done well in the past. This doesn't mean the investment will carry you all the way to retirement, but it also doesn't mean that it will tank.

Another common error under the law of small numbers is assuming that, if an event occurs a few times in a row, it won't happen the next time.[62] This kind of thinking happens in Vegas all the time: if a pair of die lands on an odd number five times in a row, many assume that the next roll will be even. They think it has to be. Six times is just too many! But this assumption isn't true. The odds of rolling an odd or even number are the same for each individual roll. Therefore, if you think the market is going to drop soon because it's been doing really well for ten years in a row (it can't go on like this forever!), then you may be falling under the spell of the law of small numbers. More evidence is needed to figure out what's going to happen with the market. And even then, given that the market is unpredictable, it's nearly impossible to be sure. (Of course, eventually the die will land on an even number; the point is that you can't accurately predict *when*.)

It's hard to be on guard and solve for every single shortcut or bias you could use. Just know that as long as you doubt your own knowledge in a healthy, non-self-defeating way, then you'll seek out enough information, avoid overconfidence, and circumvent many of the other pitfalls that lead to bad investment decisions.

Strategic Rules that Minimize Poor Investment Decision-Making and Maximize Confidence

People set rules for themselves. It's what we do. Go for a run four times a week. No TV for an hour before bed. Wash your hands as soon as you walk through the front door. Those types of rules.

Why do we set rules? It's not because we enjoy limitations. We set rules because if we don't, we'll end up where we don't want to be. It's hard to be fit. It's hard to get a good night's sleep, and it's hard to stay virus-free. Rules are handy and keep us on track.

It takes a lot of time and energy to learn Decision Science and to follow the advice laid out earlier in this chapter. This advice is valuable and necessary, but to *really* be successful at investing—to *truly* make confident investment decisions—it's important to supplement your self-awareness and self-improvement with a set of strategic rules. You'll learn more about these rules throughout the book, but for now, it's enough just to know what they are.

1. *Align your investment strategy with your life goals.* It's not enough to amass as much wealth as possible for retirement. You have some life to live before then and financial needs that have to be met. Plus, when you retire, you may not spend that much, so being a millionaire may not be necessary. Figure out what you want and need in the short-term, the long-term, and in between. Figure out what you want to leave to your family members when you go. Envision how you see yourself spending your retirement years. Knowing these life goals makes it much more possible to design an investment strategy that will *work* for you.

2. *Think of your investments as a source of income, not a source of returns.* You may feel great about a stock you own because you're getting great returns. You may feel less excited about other stock because the returns aren't as great. However, if you only focus on returns as you buy and sell, you're missing the big picture. It's not just about how much your stocks are yielding, but also about how many shares you own. In some circumstances, many shares of weaker-performing stock can yield more income than a few shares of stronger stock. Keep your eye on the big picture. Keep your focus

on the overall earnings of your portfolio, not on individual stock performance.

3. *Diversify both offensively and defensively.* Some investment vehicles are meant to earn you income (like stocks and bonds). These investments are part of your offensive strategy; they're designed to help you earn aggressively. But if you only diversify within your stock-and-bond portfolio, you can be left vulnerable, because all of your investments correlate with market performance. This means if the market crashes, so do your investments. Diversify further by including a defensive component to your strategy: investments that don't earn aggressively but still earn and are there in case the market fails. Life insurance falls into this category. It's not correlated with the market, so even if the market plummets, some of your investments remain protected. Other defensive strategies will be covered later in the book.

4. *Re-visit, re-assess, and re-allocate regularly.* A "set it and forget it" approach to investing is common but not ideal. As the market changes over time, the values of different investment tools will shift, meaning your portfolio will change. You may start out with a conservative investment portfolio, but as the values of investments change, it could be a riskier one in five to ten years. When you re-assess your portfolio every few years, do so as though you're creating it from scratch all over again. Don't just re-allocate between

vehicles you already own. New vehicles might suddenly be an option. Policies and regulations can change. Look at all options with fresh eyes, so you don't miss anything.

Each of these rules align with common decision-making mistakes that investors make. Following them can help you avoid potential decision-making pitfalls, decreasing your chances of making bad investment choices. You can use these rules as your strategic framework for investing. Then, as you make decisions, use the five mindset practices to keep your decision-making free from the influence of internal limitations (like the tendency to be impulsive or to use mental shortcuts and biases) or external constraints (like the tendency to be swayed by norms and culture).

Remember that investing with confidence doesn't mean you'll have zero doubt about your investment decisions. It just means you'll face the inherent uncertainty of investing head-on, seeing reality for what it is, and being armed to deal with it.

Now let's look at some common types of investment mindsets, why they lead to sub-optimal decisions, and how a mindset reset can lead to a less vulnerable and more confident investment portfolio.

CHAPTER 4

THE "MORE IS BETTER" INVESTOR

There once was a man with a lot of gold that he kept hidden in a secret hole in his garden. Every so often he went out to that hole, dug up the gold, counted it, and covered it up again.

He never took any of it out. He never spent any of it. He simply took pleasure in knowing it was there.

What he didn't know was that a thief had secretly been watching him count his gold from a distance. At first, this thief didn't know what the man was doing, but in time he realized there was a lot of gold in that hole. So of course, being a thief, he snuck into the garden late at night, dug up the gold, and fled.

The next day, the man went out to his garden only to find the hole had been dug up and emptied. He was devastated. A neighbor, noticing the man was panicked and distraught, went to him and asked what happened.

"My gold!" said the man. "It's all gone! Someone has stolen my gold!"

"Your gold was here, in this hole?" said the neighbor.

"Yes. I kept it right here," said the man.

The neighbor was perplexed. "Why did you keep it in a hole in the ground? Why didn't you keep it somewhere more accessible, in case you needed to spend it?"

"Spend it?!" cried the man. "I wasn't going to spend it! I was keeping it!"

The neighbor thought for a moment. Then he picked up a large stone and placed it in the hole. "There," he said. "Cover that up and keep it instead. It's worth as much as the gold you lost."

Anyone serious about investing should take the moral of this Aesop fable to heart: money has no value unless you make use of it. Yet too often, when I ask people about their financial goals or what they hope to do with the money they earn from investing, their explanation sounds much like the miser in the fable. They want to save as much as they can, invest as much as possible, and "make a lot of money" so they'll have "plenty for retirement," and do all the things or have all the things they've always wanted.

Unfortunately, many investors can't get more specific than that. Without an idea of what to spend their investment savings on, most people see their earnings as little more than something to count, feel good about, and set aside. This can be a problem, because if you don't know what you want to spend your earnings on, you won't make the best investment decisions.

When You Don't Know What You're Investing for, or If What You're Investing for Isn't Authentically Valuable to You, Your Investment Choices May as Well Be Arbitrary

Vishal and Jess are professionals in their forties who together earn more than $250K a year. They've been married for about ten years and have one son. They have a single financial goal: save all they can for retirement. Every spare dollar goes into their 401K, investments, or some other form of retirement savings. Moreover, every choice they make is designed to minimize the amount they spend now, so they'll have more to invest and spend later, and to pass on to their son. For example, they could live in a larger or newer house, but they've opted for a small, cramped one.

Though they enjoy travel, they've decided to staycation only so they can save money. They are frugal, careful, and committed. And it's working.

Their nest egg has been growing steadily since they began investing about five years ago. Their wealth advisor told them they're doing the right thing by investing as much as they can now, so they can bear the fruits of it later; he consistently applauds them for pouring all their extra hard-earned cash into a portfolio he set up for them—a portfolio that, according to him, will earn them plenty of money to spend on whatever they want when they retire at sixty-five. "You'll be multi-millionaires!" he tells them. And who wouldn't want that?

Vishal and Jess are caught up in the belief that the more they put toward their investments the better. The more they have in their retirement savings, the better off they will be because the richer they will be, and richer is better. They know most people aren't investing enough, if at all, and most Americans aren't financially prepared for retirement. By comparison, Vishal and Jess believe they're doing great.

But if you ask them what they envision for their retirement, and what their returns will be spent on, they have a hard time answering. They might say something like, "We want to retire somewhere warm," or, "We want to travel a lot." But these aren't measurable goals as much as they are vague ideas. Vishal and Jess haven't thought about how they truly hope to live once they retire. They also aren't clear about what hopes and dreams they have during the years until then, other than to work, save, and invest. This means they have no real idea of how much money they'll need or when they'll need it (whether in or before retirement). Ultimately, for them, their future seems less important than counting their money pot as it grows.

They also haven't thought about what they want for their child after they pass away. Both Vishal and Jess received little help from their own parents, so it hasn't occurred to them to think about their son's future other than paying for his college.

Vishal and Jess are not alone. Eight out of ten of my new clients can't answer this simple question: "What do you want your retirement life to look like?" Even fewer can tell me what they want their children's adult lives to look like, or what opportunities they want to leave behind for their kids.

Among those who can answer, many say they envision making purchases that come with a huge price tag, either during or before retirement. These types of goals are a variation of the "more is better" mindset. By focusing on one expensive objective, you overlook smaller goals that are more meaningful.

Take Rod and Cathy, for instance. Since they got married in

their twenties, they've had a shared vision for their retirement: become multi-millionaires, buy at least twenty acres of land in the mountains of Colorado, and build a luxury vacation home on that property. They agreed to pull no punches when it came to building the home. It would have a lot of rooms, a pool and sauna, and be constructed with only high-end materials like Italian marble. It would be the ultimate retirement home—one they could feel proud of and would represent the sum total of the hard work that got them there.

Rod and Cathy's dream came true. They currently own a beautiful $1.5 million home on a twenty-acre property in the Colorado Rockies. They were lucky. Though they both had high-paying jobs and all of their extra money funded their investments, there were no guarantees that their investments would pan out. But because they happened to retire during a time when stock prices were climbing, their earnings were substantial. If recession had hit right before their retirement, they may not have been able to realize their dream.

Unfortunately, once their home was completed, Rod and Cathy occupied it for no more than four months each year, and after two years, the couple put the house on the market. It was too remote, too cold in the winter, and too far away from amenities they didn't realize they'd miss, like medical care, grocery stores, and restaurants. Now they're waiting for someone to put down an offer, but homes like theirs get viewed about once a year, and it takes about five years or more for an offer to come through. Meanwhile, they sit and wait for the chance to own the retirement vacation home they *really* want: one that's smaller, more manageable, and located in the city.

Rod and Cathy had a clear vision of their retirement goals, and they deserve a ton of credit for making their dreams come true. But their goals weren't based on what might actually make them happy. Their goals made them feel successful and others feel envious. They reveled in sharing photographs of the home to people they knew, feeling proud of their accomplishment. They loved giving their few guests tours of their home to show it off. But ultimately, their home was built for making an impression, not for retirement.

Their home was a huge pot of gold buried in the Rocky Mountains. They could go there, see it, show it off, and feel good about having it. But when push came to shove, they preferred their modest primary residence in their hometown.

Having a goal in mind is not enough. Having a goal that sounds good when you're younger but isn't carefully thought through isn't great either. Your goal has to be the right goal, one that lines up with who you are and what brings you joy.

Many of us take the time and energy to invest, but too few of us spend any energy figuring out what's worth spending our investment earnings on. Too many of us either don't think far enough ahead, or when we do, our focus isn't realistic or clear. Without clear goals that come from a meaningful place, we may end up making investment decisions that we'll regret. Then, in that case, the best we can hope for is what Vishal and Jess probably do: go into our metaphorical garden, count up our gold, cover up the hole, and go back to our daily routines.

How Investing to Make "More" Can Cause You to End Up with Less

There are four general ways in which the mindset of investing more for its own sake can lead you down the wrong path.

First, you can max out your retirement savings for a lifestyle that doesn't require all the money you might end up saving. For example, Vishal and Jess haven't spent any time or energy considering what would make them happy in retirement. Like most people, they've gone through life doing what they've been told they should do: go to college, get a good job, marry someone nice, have children, work until retirement, and save as much as possible.

In other words, they've always gone along with the norms, without questioning whether or not the norms (in whole or in part) work for them.

What Vishal doesn't know is that if Jess were to really think about it, she would be happiest retiring in her hometown of Cincinnati, in a modest two-bedroom house close to her sister, where she could spend time with her niece and nephew—not exactly a retirement dream that requires a ton of money. Jess would also love to travel: she wants to see the Great Pyramids and go on a Caribbean cruise. But she wants to do all of that now, not when she's seventy. At seventy, she just wants to spend time with her family.

What Jess doesn't know is that Vishal wants the same thing, except he'd like to add a workshop to that modest two-bedroom home so he can spend his free time wood-working, something he's always dreamed of doing. In fact, Vishal has put this dream on hold to save for retirement. If Vishal was truly honest, he'd tell you he hates living in a cramped home. There's not even enough space for a dog, which their son really wants, and he's tired of his noisy neighbors.

Vishal and Jess both want a modest retirement. They don't need $3 million to fulfill their retirement dreams. But because Vishal and Jess don't think about their life and retirement goals, and because their wealth advisor doesn't press them to consider what they really want, they're stuck in a sub-optimal situation. They aren't aware that it's possible to have the life and retirement they want, if they would only shift their mindset away from "more is better."

A second and related problem is that when you over-save for retirement, you under-prepare for the present or near future. Though Vishal and Jess are single-mindedly focused on their returns every single day, they've put off thinking about spending their earnings into the far future. They've saved for their son's college tuition, but beyond this, they don't expect to have any major expenses until retirement. Given their circumstances, it's possible for them to contribute to an investment vehicle designed with a five- or ten-year payoff, use those earnings to upgrade to a more comfortable home, and still have more than enough for retirement. These short-term earnings can also come in handy to help their son buy his first car or home, or to even help out with expenses for their grandkids.

When you focus too hard on the finish line, you may lose sight of everything that can happen before then, and you forego spending before retirement simply because your money is buried in the garden. Or, if more immediate needs arise, you won't have a plan for spending to accommodate them.

Third, over-saving without tying your money to anything tangible and meaningful can actually lead to over-spending. This sounds counter-intuitive, but it's been known to happen.

Tony is a wealth advisor in his thirties. Yup, I'm talking

about me. When I was a young "hot shot" investor in the early 2000s, I had a single goal: amass as much wealth as possible. And I had no plans for spending that money. I simply believed that all I needed to care about was getting more, having more, keeping more. "More is better" was my personal mantra.

Why did I believe this to be true? If you asked me back then, I couldn't tell you. I just chose to believe it. I invested almost everything I made. I regularly counted my earnings in my metaphorical garden, was happy about what I saw, and then covered up the hole.

Then I had a bad day. I mean, a seriously bad day. I was in a relationship with a woman I loved deeply, someone I thought I'd spend the rest of my life with. But suddenly, it ended, and I was a wreck. I had a lot of money because all I strived to do was make money, but I had no tangible goals associated with it. My money had no meaningful value to me.

Money was also something I believed I could always make more of, so it was easy for me to think: "I just got dumped… I'll go to Vegas!" I figured I deserved it. I was miserable and I had worked hard, so why not spend my hard-earned cash on whatever I wanted?

I went to Las Vegas and spent like crazy. I also went to Italy.

I spent money on custom suits, and when I went out with friends (which was often), I usually offered to buy rounds of drinks for all of them. Eventually, I spent $20,000 in a wave of heartache and sadness trying to get over my ex-girlfriend.

I wasn't worried about the spending, partly because I thought I'd make all that money back (the market was hot, after all), but mostly because I didn't think I was taking that money away from anything else. For example, since I didn't have a child yet, I didn't attach that money to a child's college fund. I didn't attach it to my future dream vacation home. The money I spent on suits and drinks wasn't allocated for anything else, so why not blow it? What was I really losing?

At the end of my spending binge, I felt no better about the break-up, and earning that money back turned out to be harder than I thought. Not to mention that I have a son now and I'm responsible for a beautiful human being, I realize I could have put that money away to help him pay for college or buy his first home. These were goals I didn't think about before my son was born, even though I knew I wanted children and needed to prepare for them.

When your investments aren't tied to a specific goal—when all you're doing is making money for money's sake—that money ends up meaning much less to you than its actual value, and you run the risk of letting it slip through your fingers in a string of bad decisions. I've seen it time and again.

Fourth, over-saving for retirement comes with the risk that you may not be around long enough to enjoy the fruits of your labor. Or, if you are, you may no longer have the energy to enjoy your money the way you wanted to. To give an example, a young couple who were my clients saved as much as they could for retirement. They both had good jobs and made wise spending choices. And, like the hypothetical Vishal and Jess, this couple decided to forego spending on things they would have really enjoyed, like travel, because they wanted to save up for the future.

Then the husband suffered a heart attack in his late thirties and passed away. He hadn't lived the life he wanted to live yet because he was saving that for later. His wife was left with a nice sum of investment money, but she didn't have the memories with her husband she wished she'd had, of traveling and exploring the world together.

We've all heard the saying that you need to live each day like it's your last. As a wealth advisor, I can't agree with that 100 percent. But I also believe that planning only for a large pot of gold when you don't know when to spend it or what you want to spend it on won't lead to a fulfilling life. It isn't fulfilling to plan only for the distant future.

Sure, you may have a lot of money when you're at retirement age, but if sadly, you don't make it that far or can't do what you had hoped once you get there, then what good is that money to you?

The bottom line is this: spend time thinking about what you want your money to do for you, and then find a balance between saving and enjoying your money. I'm a big fan of saving money for the short term, mid-term, *and* long term.

Though Jess and Vishal, unlike the man in the fable, plan to spend their money eventually, their savings strategy is essentially no different than the miser's: they are amassing wealth for the sake of having it. When they do start spending, they won't know how much to spend or what to spend it on. Vishal and Jess aren't connecting their wealth to anything tangible. By focusing exclusively on growing their wealth without considering their endgame, they could be making sub-optimal investment decisions and leaving money on the table.

But more importantly, they could be compromising their happiness.

Most investment advice doesn't touch on personal fulfillment, but we're going there. When life is about making money just to make money—when it's all about keeping up with the Joneses or owning the nicest things—then retirement loses its meaning. As a wealth advisor, it's my job to help people grow wealthier, but I prefer not to do so at the expense of their personal fulfillment. Money is useful only insofar as it brings joy. Otherwise, as we learned in the fable of the miser, it's no good.

The notion that "more is better" as in "the more money I pour into my investments, the better" is a fictional story that comes with potentially negative implications. And yet people hang on to that story and embrace the "invest it all" mindset.

If you ask many investment advisors why they think investing more is better than investing less, they'll say, "How can more not be better? Isn't the goal of investing and wealth management to be as wealthy as possible, especially for retirement? And isn't the path to greater wealth to invest— to use your money to make even more money?"

I can't be an investment advisor and be turned off by the idea of amassing wealth, and I'm definitely not opposed to wealth. Instead, I'm saying that by focusing only on making more money, you run the risk of actually having less overall wealth, not to mention less happiness. It sounds counterintuitive, but I see it play out every day with dozens of clients who come to me to fix their poor investment decisions.

More is not always better. And earning more wealth for no other reason than to have more wealth sets you up for a poor investment strategy.

Embrace the Idea that Money isn't Everything—and Especially Not What Society Taught Us It Is

Having money is important. We wouldn't invest if it weren't. The question is, are we seeking wealth for reasons that are meaningful to us? If not, then we may be off track. And if we don't have the right mindset, we lessen our chances of making good investment decisions, which means we compromise our wealth.

The "more is better" mindset largely rests on the fact that, in most cultures, wealth is highly valued. And this is understandable. Wealth means access to resources, which means security and the ability to pay for life's basics: you have money for shelter, food, transportation, and clothing. You can't survive without them.

Wealth can bring peace of mind that allows for better health. Money gives you a sense of control and a feeling that you can solve your problems. With this control comes less stress and a healthier life. In fact, research in epidemiology reveals that earning less money decreases your chances of living longer. People with less money have a greater chance of suffering from heart disease, stroke, cancer, and committing suicide.[63]

Beyond the basics of survival and health, wealth has other meanings in our society that we highly value. For example, we often equate wealth with happiness. As a young child growing up with little money, I imagined how happy life would be once I got rich. Money has solved many problems for me, that's for sure, but even in my early years as an investor, while I felt smart and successful, I can't say that I was happy. I've come to learn that while more money *seems* to mean more happiness in our society, it's not always truly correlated with more happiness, and research backs this up.

According to work by economist Richard Easterlin, people in wealthy countries, on average, aren't any happier than those in less wealthy countries.[64] This is true when looking at developed countries, developing ones, and even in countries that have transitioned from socialism to capitalism (in eastern Europe, for example).[65]

In fact, there's an argument for measuring a country's success not by gross domestic product (GDP) but by some measure of overall happiness. New Zealand's finance minister announced not long ago that economic performance would be a lower priority, and the country would start measuring its success by measuring mental health, child poverty, domestic violence, ethnic inequality, and environmental and economic sustainability.[66] New Zealand isn't trying to get away with anything; its economy is strong and its GDP impressive. This move was made to ensure appropriate budgeting, and to ensure government funding goes where it's needed.

The bottom line: financial wealth isn't everything.

To drive this point home even further, Easterlin's work reveals the value of wealth is relative: how much you have matters only when compared to how much other people have. In his research, Easterlin discovered that although wealthier countries aren't happier overall, wealthier people are happier than those who are less wealthy *within* each country. They're not happier because they have wealth; they're happier because others have less.

People regularly compare their wealth to that of those around them. If you're making a salary of $200,000 a year, you probably feel pretty happy about it, but only if most people around you aren't making more. In fact, research in behavioral economics has shown that most people would prefer a lower salary if others around them made less, rather than a higher salary if others made more. In other words, they'd be more likely to take $60,000 a year if others made $40,000, and less likely to take $100,000 a year if others were making $130,000. These findings hold equally true if the cost of living is relatively high or low.[67]

This research shows that people would prefer less *actual* wealth if it means more *relative* wealth. It's all about comparing how we're doing against others—further evidence that real financial success is less important than what wealth *means*.

I'll stress again that the fact that we do this is totally human.

How can we judge ourselves for socially-driven behavior when we're social creatures? We compare ourselves to others because that's what social creatures do.[68]

But unfortunately, chasing wealth with this sort of mindset can make it tougher to live a good life. The more we compare ourselves to others, the worse off we tend to be. Research conducted at Purdue points out that, at a certain income level, life satisfaction caps off. Income and happiness are correlated, with happiness going up as income increases but only to a point. Once your income rises above roughly $105,000, you won't feel any happier than you did before. At least, that's what the figure was in North America in the late 2000s. In 2018, all you need to be happy in the Caribbean is $35,000, and in New Zealand $125,000. Why these amounts? Because this is what it takes to cover the basics in each country. Beyond the basics, what else is there to worry about besides keeping up with the Joneses? The drive to earn more than others and constantly compare how you're doing against them can actually decrease happiness.[69]

Let's put it this way. Generally speaking, the people around us aren't all training to run faster than everyone else. We aren't all striving to be better spellers or be the best at vacuuming. That's because doing these things well doesn't mean much more than the fact that we can do these things well. But wealth is different.

Being wealthy means we're successful, which means we're smarter or more industrious, or that we're innovative and unique. Financially successful people are often assumed to have a host of positive characteristics they may not actually have—characteristics that are the consequence of the *halo effect*. Wealthy people may be viewed as more intelligent or industrious than those with less money, when intelligence and industriousness may have little to do with a person's financial success. It's much easier to become wealthy if your parents have money, for example.

It's also worth noting that humans attribute negative traits to people who aren't as wealthy, making poverty just as unappealing as wealth is appealing. Many people with little money overcome huge obstacles just to survive—they work hard and think outside the box in creative ways, yet they aren't recognized for their accomplishments because they don't have the dollars to show for it.

Being swept up in the social meanings surrounding wealth (and poverty) could potentially lead to bad decision-making when it comes to investing. An optimal investment mindset, one that leads to better investment decisions, focuses on how your investments will help you reach your actual goals—the goals that are directed at making you happy, rather than wealthy.

For example, if you have or plan to have children, you may

want to weigh the importance of their welfare against having millions in the bank. You may want to consider what matters to you specifically regarding the kind of lives you'd like them to live, now and after you're gone. If children aren't in your future, it's worth asking yourself what brings you true fulfillment.

As social creatures, we care about human connection and community, personal fulfillment, internal peace, and contentment. Would it be more fulfilling to spend money on your children or community now, while foregoing the millions you may receive later? Perhaps. It's up to each of us to decide what's best on an individual basis, and the decision should be thoughtfully made. If social forces (social meanings) make those decisions for us, then we won't get to where we truly deserve to be.

Exercise: Protect Yourself from Potential Mindset Pitfalls—Get Clear On Your Goals

Breaking free from the "more is better" mindset requires awareness that this mindset is exactly that: a state of mind that can be changed, not an absolute truth or tried-and-true investment principle. What wealth means is cultural, and that meaning is transient.

Making the right mindset change starts with you. You know yourself. You know what you like and what you don't like.

You know what you'll likely want to do after retirement, and you know what you absolutely don't want to do. And if you don't know, no one is in a better position to find out than you are.

Here's a goal-setting exercise that can get you going. It's designed to make you think carefully about your life, not just your retirement.

If you have a wealth advisor who has never asked you about your hopes and dreams, your long-term goals, and even your short-term goals, you may want to find a new advisor. Even if you don't plan to work with an advisor, you can't start investing until you know yourself and what you want. Here are some questions you should answer, whether you've just started investing or you're late in the game. It's never too late to adjust your strategy to meet the right objectives.

Short- and mid-term goals:

- *Where do you see yourself in the next five to ten years? In the next ten to twenty years? Specifically:*
  - *What will your career look like over the next several years? How different will it be from where you are now?*
  - *What will your living situation look like? Do you plan on moving to a bigger home or growing a family? Do*

you plan to see your kids leave home, and if so, do you plan to downsize your home? If so, what do these changes to your life look like?

- *Do you expect to pay for your children's college tuition, or otherwise help your children as they transition out of your home? Do you have children with long-term medical needs and expenses?*
- *Do you have dreams of buying vacation property, a boat, or some other high-ticket luxury item? Do you want to take significant time off work to travel the globe? Are there any other dreams or hopes you wish to fulfill in the near or mid-term?*
- *What kinds of hobbies, sports, or activities do you expect to participate in? How risky are they, and how much of your time do you plan to spend on them? How much money will it cost to sustain these interests?*
- *Is there any reason why your expectations for the near future may not be met? For example, are you worried about job security, the economy, a sudden decision to have a child, etc.?*

Long-term/ post-retirement goals:

- *At what age do you and your spouse ideally hope to retire?*
- *Once you retire, what do you imagine the first five years of your retirement to look like? Would you simply stay at home and relax? Do you want to stay low-key for a few years and simply rest while you plan your retirement adventure? Or*

do you want to immediately do exciting things like travel or pick up an exciting hobby?

- *How about the next five years of retirement? Is this when you'd be ready to check items off your bucket list? Or will you be winding down, hoping to have everything checked off by now?*
- *During the course of your retirement, where do you hope to live? Be specific: what country, state, city, and area do you have your sights set on? Would this require moving? If so, how many times do you expect to move during retirement?*
- *What specific daily activities do you hope to engage in? Are you looking forward to spending a lot of time at home reading or gardening? Is your hope to learn how to fly a plane or sail a boat? Is your dream to pour yourself into volunteer work? Do you plan on traveling a lot, or starting a new business?*
- *Do you have dreams of spending money to help your children or grandchildren while you're in retirement? If so, how? Will you help pay for college? Will you help them buy a bigger home? Or something else?*
- *Do you have any medical issues that you need to plan around as you think about your life goals? What expenses might be associated with such issues?*
- *Finally, out of all your retirement goals, which ones are "must haves" and which are "delights?" In other words, are there any you forgo without feeling regret? Which ones must you do to feel you've lived the life you've wanted?*

You can maximize your chances of making great investment decisions when you align your goals with the right objectives and the right strategy.

Once you have your goals laid out, you need to figure out how you will accomplish them. One of the most important lessons every investor should learn are the differences between an investment goal, an objective, and a strategy. It might seem obvious enough, but it's easy to confuse these three in application. Get it right, and you can invest with confidence. Get it wrong, and you could scramble when things go south, reacting to bad situations rather than proactively preparing for them.

How Goals, Objectives, and Strategy Fit Together

Goals, objectives, and strategy fit together. Goals are what you ultimately want to accomplish, or what you'd like to happen. They include retirement goals like how you want to spend your time or where you want to live. They also include shorter-term goals, like buying a home in ten years or taking an expensive vacation next summer. Objectives break down exactly what you need to accomplish in order to meet your goals. You can't, for example, decide to buy a house in ten years and then expect to automatically pull it off. You need to take steps to get there, like save money for a down payment, which involves knowing how much you expect your future home to cost.

Nika and I are using "strategy" here as synonymous with "plan." These are actual, tactical things you can start doing now to make sure you hit your objectives and your goals. To save up enough money for your home, you need to make choices about how much to set aside each month, what other types of spending you can reduce in order to save up enough, etc.

	DEFINITION	EXAMPLE
GOAL	The ultimate thing you want	A vacation home in ten years
OBJECTIVES	Measurable things you can do that will directly get you to your goal	Decide where you want your vacation home to be (country, city, neighborhood)
		Decide what kind of home you want (condo or house)
		Gather pricing information on homes that are similar to what you want
		Estimate value of home (with inflation) in ten years
		Ensure that in ten years you have 20 percent of that estimated value in savings, through a set of investment and savings decisions
STRATEGY	How you plan on accomplishing your objectives	Set aside 30 percent of your earnings to save toward your home, the rest for retirement or other goals
		Invest a third of that 30 percent in high-return, higher-risk stocks
		Invest two-thirds in whole life, with guaranteed returns uncorrelated to the market

A great way to understand the difference between goals, objectives, and strategies—and why they matter—is by analogy. We'll use professional athletes as our example. Every athlete is in it to win. Ask them what they hope to achieve in their careers, and they'll most likely say "to be the best" or "to win." They train hard every day, many of them putting their physical well-being on the line, because winning is their goal.

But athletes generally can't just go out and win. They need to do certain things to get there. They need to have great cardiovascular conditioning, so they can meet their objectives regarding how many miles they're able to run and at what pace. Or they may need to be strong, so they can meet their objectives for how much weight they can lift. They also may need to perfect the techniques of their sport, so they can meet their objectives for specific techniques they have to work on.

These specific things athletes need to accomplish are their objectives, and all of their objectives should ladder up to their ultimate goal. Otherwise, they'll get off track and risk not meeting their goal, which is to win. For instance, you can't win at soccer if all you do is bicep curls at the gym. You can't win at body building if all you do is run.

As an investor, what you envision for your life in the immediate, mid-term, and long-term future is your goal. If you did the goal-setting exercise earlier, you should have a list of your goals in front of you, short and mid-term, and for post-retirement. Goals are necessary but they can be difficult to reach if you don't establish the steps you need to get there. Your retirement goal might be to "live in a riverfront home in the Colorado Rockies," but most of us can't make that happen without some tangible steps. *Objectives are those steps.*

For instance, one objective might be to save enough money for a down payment. To know how much to save, you need to estimate the value of the home you want to buy. Once you have that dollar amount, then you have a clear objective: you know how much you need and when you'll need it. Of course, life throws curve balls, and things can change, such as your income or housing prices, but you will still have a close enough idea of what's needed.

Exercise: Create Objectives Aligned with Your Goals

Goals are difficult to reach if you don't take small steps to get there. Objectives are the smaller, incremental steps you need to take to ultimately reach your goal. Defining your objectives takes some time and some thinking.

I'd like you to start thinking through your objectives for the investment goals you have. Select two to three goals that you came up with in the first goal-setting exercise. For each goal, ask yourself the following questions:

- *How much research do I need to do to learn what it takes to actually (and realistically) achieve my goal? Do I know what is involved in reaching that goal?*
  - *For example, if your goal is to learn how to fly a helicopter, do you know what that requires? Do you know what steps you need to take to get a license to fly, including how many classes you need to take and how much airtime you need to clock? Do you know whether or not you need to buy your own helicopter, or if you can rent them? If you don't know what it takes to reach that goal, then you need to do more research.*
  - *If your goal is to buy a vacation home on a remote beach, do you know which locations are ideal for the lifestyle you want? Do you know what real estate is available, and if the real estate you're interested in is near amenities, resources, or entertainment you can't live without?*
- *Do you know how much money you'll need to reach each goal? If not, make finding the answer part of your research, and then estimate the amount to the best of your ability.*
- *Once you've done all the necessary information-gathering and have ballpark costs for each goal, document all the steps that are required to reach that goal, and then place them in chronological order. How long will each step take? These are your objectives.*
- *Nothing's certain, and things might change in your life or in the world. These changes could impact whether or not you can meet each objective. Are there any particular events that could affect your reaching your objective, either in a*

positive or negative way? For instance, might a relative pass away and leave you part of their estate? Might your spouse lose their job, leaving you with less income than expected? Or is it possible that your health might require you to stay close to an urban area near good doctors, rather than on a remote beach?

- *If any changes occur, how might your objectives change? What are your Plan B objectives?*
- *How much additional money would you need for Plan B?*

Once you have a set of objectives, you can lay out a strategy for reaching them. Your strategy is *how* you'll achieve what you hope to achieve. For example, to have enough money to put down on a home in a nearby gated retirement community, you can pull cash from your savings account, liquidate some assets (including stocks), or sell your current home. You can do a combination of these things spread out over time or do something different altogether, such as refinancing part of your home and investing that amount to make more money. Whatever your strategy, unless it's tied directly to an objective, you are less likely to reach your goal.

How do you know you have the right strategy? This is where a solid understanding of investment options comes in. Stocks, bonds, annuities, life insurance, real estate, even a simple savings account—each option is uniquely designed to help you fulfill a specific set of objectives. None are one-size-fits-all, but there are general rules you can turn to regarding the objectives that each option can help you meet. The more you learn about what each investment can and can't do, the better equipped you'll be to build the right strategy.

For example, if it's in your five-year plan to buy your first home, you don't want the design of your stock investment portfolio to maximize returns for retirement. You want to earn enough for a down payment on your home in five years, so you need to invest accordingly.

If your only plan is to retire modestly with a new vacation home and leave your children with at least a million dollars each, then a life insurance policy might be something to consider. Such a policy will make sure your children are taken care of while also providing a source of extra cash if you need it in the meantime.

You'll need to regularly revisit your strategy and objectives over time to make sure they're still most closely aligned with your goals. It's important to do your research and to consider talking to an investment strategist like myself— someone who knows more than just stocks and can offer a holistic approach to get you as close to realizing your personal objectives as possible.

Sometimes your objectives and goals are aligned in the beginning, but over time as things change (which they will), you'll need to reassess what you really want in life. For example, getting married or having a child when you didn't expect to are major life events that often shift goals and expectations. If you don't regularly check in with your goals, objectives, and strategy, you run the risk of retiring in bad shape or not having the finances you need along the way.

Here's another sports analogy to illustrate the importance of revisiting your goals, objectives, and strategy. Tony Hawk, arguably the best professional skateboarder ever, essentially admitted to experiencing a disconnect between his goal and his objectives in the documentary, *The Bones Brigade*.[70] He was at the top of the sport, to a degree that few athletes before or since have ever known. He clocked countless hours of practice, pushing himself to constantly create new moves and do his old moves even better.

And Tony won. A lot. He was so unparalleled as a skater that it got to where he was expected to win at each competition, and anything less was unacceptable. The pressure was immense, and he succumbed to it. He was solely preoccupied with winning.

But deep down he wanted to enjoy what he was doing. Joy is what got him hooked, and joy is what he wanted to keep experiencing, but winning wasn't bringing him joy. In fact, he began to hate skating. He felt heavy-hearted and considered quitting. His objective (winning) didn't help him reach his goal (joy). And his training strategy was tied only to winning, which made joy even less possible.

All Tony wanted to do was create new moves, try new things, and push boundaries. All he wanted to do was innovate.

So Tony let go of his old objective and found a new one, along with a new strategy to accompany it. Instead of heading into each competition with the objective of winning, Tony went out with the objective of having fun. He changed his strategy, and in doing so he went from wanting to walk away from the sport completely to falling in love with it all over again. He re-discovered his bliss by abandoning the objective and strategy that wasn't getting him there.

And he still won. A lot.

You can change your objectives. Just be sure to remember money is a means to "something else." Your investment returns are meaningful and optimized only if they're tied to a deeper goal or endgame. That endgame is totally personal and up to you. But you need goals, and you need clear ones. You also need steps (objectives) that ladder up to each goal. And every investment option you choose, whether stocks, annuities, real estate, or futures, should be a thoughtful choice designed specifically to reach your objective.

As I said before, this process won't guarantee you'll hit a specific dollar amount before you retire. There are no guarantees with investing, and uncertainty is the only thing that's certain. But if you choose to let go of the "more is better" mindset (especially the "more for the sake of having more" mindset), you'll invest with confidence. You'll invest in a way that optimizes your potential earnings and protects you as much as possible from whatever life throws your way.

CHAPTER 5

THE "INVEST IN THE HOTTEST TRENDS" INVESTOR

Richard is thirty-one years old and a day trader. His wife earns a decent income as a therapist, making enough money to support both of them. Richard recently lost his job at a bank and decided to try day trading while waiting for his next gig. He enjoyed it so much that it became his full-time job.

As a day trader, Richard wakes up early to get a jump on market behavior right away. He monitors sales and purchases to see which stocks are moving and which ones aren't. He buys stocks that increase in value more rapidly than others, and as stocks he owns start to decline, he sells them. From early morning through the afternoon, he's glued to his computer screen, watching what everyone is doing and deciding accordingly.

Richard spends his days following bandwagons. Wherever a bandwagon goes, Richard goes. He learns what the bandwagon does through blogs, news stories, and television shows. Through these resources, he hears experts talk about what's hot, and Richard concludes that because everyone is doing something, it must be worth doing.

If the bandwagon says, "Jump on that stock!" he jumps. He's under the spell of the *bandwagon effect*.[71] No one gives him solid information with which to weigh the pros and cons—all he knows is how many people are doing the thing he's considering.

If I were to press Richard to consider a more optimal strategy, he'd resist. Even though my years of experience demonstrate financial success for my clients, Richard would rather hop on the bandwagon. He, like many investors, is convinced that investing is a crap shoot, so why not do what everyone else is doing? And after all, isn't the majority usually correct? Besides, if you aren't doing what everyone else is doing, you could be missing out on a hot opportunity.

This brings us to a psychological by-product of the bandwagon effect: the "fear of missing out" (FOMO).[72] FOMO matters because it adds to the stress of the inherent uncertainty in investing, creating a sense of urgency to do what everyone else is doing. I've seen FOMO play out time and again among investors, and I can't blame them. It's hard to know what to do when it comes to investing and, given there's so much market insecurity, it's no wonder people seek security in numbers.

But unfortunately, if people don't stop and think about what they're doing, they could be compromising their investments.

The Bandwagon Effect Is Powerful, but It Isn't the Foundation for Healthy, Stress-Free Investing

Abby, like Richard, is a day trader, and she gets excited when stocks pop out at her like shiny objects. She finds out about new companies when investors suddenly purchase shares quickly. She doesn't do a lot of research about any company. She doesn't learn about their profitability, roadmap, or leadership style. She's simply captivated by stocks that are new to her and moving quickly.

Her investment behavior looks something like this: she buys shares in stocks that look promising, but if she learns that another company's shares are quickly being snatched up by other investors, she worries that she's missing out on a huge opportunity. So she chooses to purchase some shares of that stock, too. But to afford this purchase, she sells shares of a different stock she bought last week. In another week, this cycle happens all over again. After a few months, she's hopped all over the place from stock to stock, hoping to hit the jackpot but never sticking around long enough for real earnings to come in.

FOMO can be an incredibly emotional experience. It's wrought with anxiety, restlessness, and worry. It stems partly from concerns that others are experiencing joys or successes that you aren't. It's why social media sites may have a negative impact on mental health.[73] When we engage with social media, we see all the wonderful things everyone else is doing and what we might be missing out on. If we see investment-related news in our feeds, we wonder what we're losing by not hopping on the bandwagon. This worry causes psychological stress and increases anxiety and depression, causing even the most rational decision-maker to rashly choose poor options just to feel good again.

Even if it's only temporary.

People under the spell of FOMO are constantly susceptible to the bandwagon effect. They find it difficult to come up with an investment strategy tied to their goals because they're convinced there's something better that they're missing. They don't stick to an investment long enough to reap any rewards. Ironically, their worry about missing out leads them to miss out.

It's worth noting the other side of the bandwagon effect, which is the *underdog effect*. This happens when you go *against* the majority for the specific reason of going against the majority.[74] People under the spell of the underdog effect reject the bandwagon. Though research on the underdog effect and decision-making is less conclusive, those who prefer underdog investments are equally likely to make sub-optimal choices. Choosing to go against the crowd only for the sake of going against the crowd isn't any more rational or maximizing than getting on the bandwagon. And when it comes to investing, rooting for the underdog can hurt.

For example, Nika knew someone who invested most of their savings in a tech company that was cool and edgy but had a hard time competing against the giants in its category. Its stocks hadn't been performing, and there was no indication they'd turn around soon. Why did this investor choose to pour all of his money into this bad investment? "Because I want to support the little guy," he said, "and I believe in what they're doing."

What happened to his investment money? He lost it all. And in the end, his financial show of support didn't help the underdog company one bit.

There's a Feeling of Safety in Numbers—but Safety Doesn't Always Mean Strong Returns

People usually hop on a bandwagon because a bandwagon can feel secure. They usually don't do the research or crunch the numbers, and they conclude bandwagon behavior is really the most beneficial for them. People who jump on a bandwagon can be very different from one another, with different preferences, tastes, and goals. But as we join the crowd, we don't think about whether everyone else's goals are like ours, or if we share the same objectives. We just assume that if most people are doing something, they must know what they're doing.

But what works for the majority may not work for you. In fact, what the bandwagon is doing may not be working for most people who are on that bandwagon.

At one time or another, we've all held the belief that the majority must have a point. If you've ever tried to learn something new on Wikipedia, then you've decided that majority opinion can't be all wrong. But when it comes to investing, where everyone should have an investment plan custom-tailored to their specific circumstances, following the crowd can come with negative consequences.

Bandwagons take time to gain momentum. By the time a hot investment is bought up by the bandwagon, it loses its potential to make money for investors. The bandwagon can actually *cause* investments to lose value, even when the bandwagon appears to be backing the best investments.

We can compare the bandwagon to the world of fashion. Hot trends in fashion are usually introduced by people who are on the cutting edge. Those "in the know" wear what's hot. Fashion magazines feature these trends, and eventually celebrities are seen wearing them. As trends get more exposure, consumers start to catch on. When the trend hits critical mass—the point where enough people adopt it and make it mainstream—those on the cutting edge abandon the trend because it's now too common. While these fashionistas move on to the next cutting-edge trend, the majority on the bandwagon are stuck with a style they wear for the next few years, past the point of its trendiness.[75]

By adopting a trend, the bandwagon kills the trend.

The same goes for investments, particularly stocks. The best time to buy a stock is when it's undervalued: when the selling price is lower than what the stock is actually worth. If you can buy an undervalued stock, you're getting a bargain. It's like buying a brand-new SUV for $5,000, or a brand-spanking new home for $50,000. Who wouldn't jump on that? The problem is, undervalued stocks are hard to identify. Money managers who are constantly on top of the market are better suited to finding these gems than the average do-it-yourself investor, but they still have to work to discover them.

Once these stocks are discovered, they're "hot." Once they become hot, most investors want a piece. Can you blame them? If brand new cars were being sold down the street for as low as $5,000, wouldn't you expect everyone in the neighborhood to check them out, if not buy one?

Just like a majority catching wind of undervalued cars flock to the car lot, so do investors chase after stocks that are worth more than their ticket price. As news about each hot stock gets out through web sites, blogs, podcasts, and TV "experts," more people buy it. Suddenly, enough people are buying that stock that others start to believe it's a good buy, just because everyone else is buying it.

Suddenly, there's a bandwagon.

But here's the catch: you only benefit if you're in on the deal early. A lot of people don't get in on the deal early because they're following the majority, and the majority hasn't caught wind of it yet. Buying these undervalued stocks may feel too risky when you don't have the majority behind you.

But as more people catch on and buy that stock, the stock price goes up. And as more people buy it, the more expensive it becomes. When purchasing the stock becomes bandwagon behavior, the stock is no longer undervalued. It's no longer the deal it was when it was hot, and it's no longer worth tripping over yourself to buy. The thing that made the stock worth buying (the fact that it was a deal) no longer exists, specifically because bandwagon behavior extinguished it. In fact, it might become the *opposite* of a deal once the bandwagon gets ahold of it. You could end up buying high when you should be buying low.

In short, when it comes to investing, doing what the majority does may mean you're already too late to the game. Not always, but the risk is great with the bandwagon, so if you only keep your eye on what others are doing without evaluating your options independently, you could make sub-optimal investment decisions. You're essentially wearing that trend from two seasons ago when you should be looking ahead to what may be fresh next season.

You Don't Want to Be on the Bandwagon When It Turns into a Sinking Ship

Following the bandwagon may also lead to hanging on to assets longer than you should, which means selling low when you should be selling high. As we mentioned before, bandwagons have their own momentum. They carry their own inertia. Just as we generally hop on an investment bandwagon when it's too late, we can hop off too late also.

Todd's story is a good example. Todd saw an opportunity to invest in a pharmaceutical company that was researching a new medication poised to fill an unmet need in the market. His decision to buy was sound: he did his research, found out what the company's stock was valued, how likely it was for this new medication to hit the market soon, how promising the medication was, and how strong the market fit for the product. He suspected the company would make quite a bit of money from this new medicine, and he surmised that its profits would increase the value of the company. Todd knew there was no crystal ball and no guarantees, but having conducted his due diligence, he invested in the company with confidence.

Soon after the new medicine entered the market, sales boomed, the company's profits skyrocketed, and the company got a lot of press attention. Others wanted to get in on the stock while the getting was still good and started buying up shares. As they did, the value of the stock increased.

Todd was ecstatic. He had bought low, and as he saw the share prices increase, he knew his returns would be huge.

At this point, Todd wondered if he should sell. If he did, he could make a substantial profit, then turn around and invest that profit in another company with undervalued stock. But he was uncertain, so he hesitated. He decided to wait and see what the market would do. He thought, *if enough people start to sell their shares, then I will, too.*

Basically, Todd flinched. He lost confidence in his decision-making, and his uncertainty caused him stress. He did what his stress compelled him to do, which was to do nothing. Since the majority was doing nothing, he believed he should do nothing as well. Even as the stock's value plateaued, he did nothing, because no one else made a move.

Suddenly, the company suffered from a series of unforeseen scandals involving embezzlement and accounting fraud. And just as suddenly, investors lost confidence in the company and started selling their shares. The bandwagon was letting go of their shares, so Todd sold, too. But by the time he sold, his shares had declined in value to the point where his profits were much lower than they would have been had he sold earlier, when the company was performing strongly. He did well to buy low, but rather than selling high, he followed the bandwagon and sold at a mediocre price.

There are no guarantees because you can't predict the future, but a safer choice for Todd would have been to ignore the bandwagon and make a decision to optimize his chances of meeting his objectives.

Bandwagons and FOMO can also lead to other problems. If

you're susceptible to FOMO and constantly on the lookout for bandwagons, you may not let your investments mature enough to be of value. In order for most investments to pay off, you have to do more than put money into them. You also have to put in the right amount of time.

Not every investment requires a long-term commitment. Sometimes you might want to invest with a high-risk strategy specifically to try for a short-term return. But sometimes you want to stick with something long enough for it to count, and FOMO doesn't allow you to do that. Stocks increase and decrease in value all the time, and if you look at their performance over the short term, they appear volatile. But if you look at stock market performance over the span of one, five, or ten years, they look a lot more promising.

FOMO causes people to jump before their investments pay off. Similar behavior is described with online dating: a person with FOMO is less likely to get to know individual people and more likely to hop from one date to the next, due to fear that there's someone better. Meanwhile, they don't put in the time and energy necessary to get to know anyone or to find out who might be right for them. In the same way, FOMO investors can hop around so much that they lose more than they earn.

We Follow Because We Feel Unknowledgeable on Our Own—Fight That Feeling and You'll Make Better Investment Decisions

Having perfect information about investment choices is impossible. Having information about the future is a pipe dream. This makes us lose confidence in our decisions, which stresses us out. To alleviate that stress, we seek out any bit of real information we can find—tangible information that doesn't force us to guess and data we can sink our teeth into. With most bandwagon decisions, we follow the majority because we feel we don't have enough information.

We see this happen often with voting behavior, too.[76] Most people who vote in political elections don't *really know* each candidate. Think about the last presidential election: if you voted (or even if you didn't), you had some opinion about the candidates, and that opinion was based on information you sought out or came across. You may have learned a lot about each candidate. You may have tried your hardest to uncover every fact, insight, and juicy detail, and you may have learned a lot.

But the truth is, information about political candidates isn't easily available. You can't know candidates the same way you know your neighbor or co-worker. Most of the time, you only find out a slice about the candidates you pay attention to, and when it comes to most local politicians, you may know even less. In King County, Washington, you can vote for "District Court, Shoreline Electoral District, Judge

Position 1." Many people living in Shoreline probably can't tell you who holds that position, much less what kind of person they are.

It's not impossible to learn about candidates up for election nationally or locally, but unless you know a candidate personally, it's hard to know them *well*. And if you want to cast your vote for a politician who's trustworthy, hardworking, and has integrity, your best (if not only) option is to look for clues that point to these traits, because hard evidence might be difficult to find.

And who the majority supports is one of those clues.

Research has revealed that public opinion polls have an impact on who people vote for.[77] A candidate with majority support is considered more desirable, and this perception alone can lead to many votes for that candidate. Another factor is how well a candidate did in previous elections—this is a way to gauge how popular they are. All of this suggests the actual policies or character of a candidate may matter much less than majority opinion.

Voting for a candidate is sort of like making an investment decision. The benefits of actual investment vehicles or the long-term value of various stocks could play less of a role in decision-making than what everyone else is doing. You might have a sense about each of your options, but each option—whether a candidate or an investment asset—can behave in unexpected ways after you select them. To make a confident decision, you need to gather as much information as possible to predict what will happen. With candidates, we want to know if they mean what they say, and if they will stick to their word. With investing, we want to know if our investments will pay off, or if they'll let us down.

But information is sparse, and the future is uncertain. Therefore, people, in a very human and understandable way, rely on the bandwagon as a decision-making shortcut. Rather than struggle with selecting the best option and not having enough information to do so, why not just do what everyone else is doing?

Sometimes "everyone else" can be a group of friends. I worry about clients who belong to investment clubs, whether formal or informal. People in these clubs pool their money together and make investment decisions as a group. In theory, this sounds like a great idea. It can give people an opportunity to meet other investors and learn from them and to benefit from group knowledge. It always feels better to invest with others who have an interest in the outcome and who are right there with you as you try to make the best decisions with your money.

But behavioral economists have found investment clubs to be problematic. In clubs where there's pressure to conform, people won't challenge each other much, and the loudest voice in the room often gets their way. Even when that loudest voice isn't the smartest, the urge to not rock the boat causes people to hop on the bandwagon. Decisions made by these investment groups generally aren't good ones, and many people who join these clubs lose money.[78]

It's also important to note that poor psychological and emotional wellness can exacerbate the bandwagon effect. Stress can practically throw people into a state of FOMO. Psychological research has revealed that in times of worry, stress, or fear, people are more likely to do what they know the majority is doing. This is because these emotions accompany high levels of uncertainty. For example, in one study led by marketing professor Vladas Griskevicius of the University of Minnesota,[79] research participants were divided into two groups. Half were shown a scary scene from the movie *The Shining*, where Jack Nicholson's character tried to kill his wife and son, while the other half watched Ethan Hawke and Julie Delpy fall for each other in the romantic film *Before Sunrise*.

Then, viewers in both groups were shown two ads for a museum and asked which one did a better job of urging them to visit the museum. One of the ads tried to appeal to potential visitors by stating the museum was "visited by over a million people each year," while the second message stated visiting the museum would make you "stand out from the crowd." In other words, the first message was about doing what everyone else does, while the second message was about doing something unique.

Those who viewed the scene from *The Shining* were more convinced by the "visited by a million people" message than those who viewed *Before Sunrise*. This suggests that being subjected to fear-triggering events can make people want to go along with the crowd. Being subjected to fear-triggering events made participants want to go along with the crowd. When things feel tough, we lean toward following the majority.

Investing is tough and scary. Maybe not as scary as Jack Nicholson in *The Shining* but arguably scary enough to trigger the need for security in the majority.

If FOMO is plaguing you, then it's important to stay in touch with your emotions as you decide what to invest in. FOMO comes with a lot of anxiety. If you are anxious about your investments, constantly checking their performance, and feeling sweaty and nervous about what you see, that's a bad sign. If your heart races as you make investment choices and you feel a little obsessive about your portfolio, then you may be making bad decisions. If you decide impulsively, or feel an incredible amount of relief immediately after a sale or purchase only to feel anxious soon afterwards, then FOMO may be compromising your ability to accumulate wealth. You're more susceptible to the bandwagon effect, more influenced by what everyone else is doing, and less likely to do what's truly best for you.

With FOMO, it's tough to be confident about who to vote for when you don't know what most people think, and it's difficult to make investment decisions without knowing what most others are doing. We rely on the behavior of the majority because we believe there is safety in numbers. And when it comes to investing, we desperately need that safety. I've had clients tell me they're investing in tech because "that's what everyone else is doing." Some clients pour all their extra savings into real estate because "everyone says the market is hot right now." Other investors have told me that their primary indicator for deciding what stocks to purchase is how they've performed in the recent past because "if prices are high, then a lot of people think it's valuable, so I should invest in it."

We may not be able to predict how our investments will do in the future, but we can be certain where most people are putting their investment dollars right now. And we guess that if everyone else is doing it, they must be onto something. If that many people are making a specific decision, they can't all be wrong.

But they *can* be wrong. And even if they're doing what turns out to be best for them, your goals and objectives may be different from theirs. Which means your strategy must be custom-tailored, not one-size-fits-all.

Think of Your Earnings as Income, Not Returns

Bandwagons are appealing because everyone is on them, and it's hard to be the odd man out. It's hard to convince yourself that you know what's best, and your situation is different enough to be handled differently, or that you'll be OK if everyone else makes big, fast money and you don't. But if you blindly follow the pack, you could miss meeting your life goals. You could end up not being able to afford your kid's college tuition, retiring later than you want, or worse.

So how can you shift your mindset to where you're comfortable enough to go against the majority if necessary? In my experience, investors who focus on the bandwagon do so because they wonder what the majority believes will yield large returns. This means the first step is to *stop focusing on your returns.*

That's right, I said it. As counterintuitive as it sounds, the best way to invest with confidence is to stop caring so much about returns.

Let's stop here for a second. Most of us have been introduced to investing by learning that it's all about the returns. This is why we invest, right? And how we choose our investments is based on whether an option is likely to yield a four, six, or 20 percent return, right?

Not necessarily. The right mindset and approach is to reset so you think about your earnings as *income* and to evaluate your investment earnings against your other sources of income. This will help you determine if you're earning enough to reach your goals.

Focusing on earnings as income involves two aspects of investing that a focus on returns alone won't reveal to you. First, it acknowledges that each return rate comes with a *likelihood*. For example, cryptocurrency investments may yield strong returns at a particular point in time, but what's the likelihood that its high return rate will be stable during the period when you invest?

If your goal is to maximize your *income*, you won't just care about how much money you'll see coming in over the immediate short-term but how much you'll make over the next one to five years. For example, an investment with a 5 percent return that is uncorrelated to the market (and is a potentially safer investment) is *more likely* to yield you a more *predictable income* over the next several years than investing in highly volatile, high-return stocks. If making more money is your goal, then you should maximize your likelihood of making that money by the time you need it, rather than focusing on how much you're making on your returns right now.

Next, a focus on income shifts your thinking to maximizing the earnings you get from your overall portfolio, not just what you earn from one specific investment vehicle, or one specific stock. When you do this, you see that investments with lower return rates could actually earn you more income than those with higher return rates, under certain conditions.

For example, company A's stock has yielded a 6 percent return over the last year while company B's return rate is 10 percent. By focusing on returns only, you might think that company B is the right choice. However, what if I told you that company A's stock is much more affordable and that you could buy up to five times the number of shares in company A than in company B? If you do the math, owning many shares of low-return stock can, in some circumstances, earn you more income than owning a smaller number of shares of high-return stock.

By considering an investment's return rate, its likelihood of stability, and its affordability in terms of the number of shares you can own, you have a better chance of generating greater income and minimizing investment risks.

Also, think about your investments holistically, as opposed to a set of distinct and unconnected purchases. Let's go back to fashion to illustrate what this means. If you've never watched a top fashion designer's runway show from start to finish, you should go online and do so. You'll see that all the clothes in a single show are connected by a common theme. A good fashion show isn't about showing off individual pieces: it's about telling a complete story with designs that fit together.

In the same way, your portfolio shouldn't be a collection of stocks you've picked up here and there for independent reasons. It should be holistic with connected parts—a complete investment plan that considers how your different purchases work together to yield the strongest returns for you.

Exercise: Do You Think Holistically about Your Income?

A few simple steps can ensure that you're approaching your investments in a holistic way, as income rather than returns. Write down all of your current financial planning vehicles. Include everything: your 401K, IRAs, stocks, life insurance, and real estate.

- *Now, for each investment, write down the return rate for each, or the current purpose it serves. If you don't know the exact return rate, try to write down if each is yielding a high, moderate, or small return. In other words, classify them.*
- *Now, altogether, do you know how much these investments are earning as part of your whole income portfolio (including income from your job)?*

- *Now, think about ways in which you could actually increase your income earnings. For example:*
  - *What if you invested less in stocks and put money toward insurance-based products? Do you know how this would impact your income over the long term? If not, how can you find out the answer to this question?*
  - *What if you harvested gains from your tech stocks and invested in less expensive, more promising stocks in other companies? How might this impact your overall portfolio? If you're not sure, what would you need to know to become sure?*
  - *What if you invested in other vehicles you haven't considered, like bonds, annuities, or even real estate? Or what if you implemented asset-protection strategies using life insurance? Can you imagine the potential benefits of your portfolio if you explored these options?*

In many circumstances, the majority knows best. But investing is so personal, and your goals so unique to you, it's hard to imagine the majority knows what will work best for *you*. Investing happens in a highly uncertain atmosphere, wrought with imperfect information, so it's not clear how a large number of people can know what will happen in the market, even if they work together.

It's not always necessary to stand out from the crowd. It's wise, however, to question if the crowd really knows *you*, and if it has your best interests in mind. And once you do, you can maximize your income and reach your goals.

CHAPTER 6

THE "DO SOMETHING" INVESTOR

Nate and his wife Pooja are young newlyweds who work at the same accounting firm. They recently bought a home and are preparing to have kids. Much of their money goes into their joint savings account—they want to be able to afford the costs of child-rearing and save for their kids' education.

Investing isn't quite a priority for them. If you ask them about their investments, they say they're fine, but all they're doing is putting the maximum amount allowed into their 401K plans. When asked if they'd diversify their investment portfolio with other vehicles, they say they don't need to. Between their 401Ks and their home, they feel covered.

They admit to knowing nothing about investing. "It stresses

me out," says Nate, and they believe "it's all a gamble anyway," so to them, they have nothing to gain by exploring more options. They suspect many people their age haven't even started investing anyway, so they feel ahead of the game.

What matters to them isn't what they're investing in—what matters is the simple fact they're investing. Younger people are more likely to embrace this point of view, maybe because they have time to see their investments grow. They don't see investing as a strategic exercise, so they don't think about how different strategies can yield different levels of returns. They do *something*, cross "invest" off their to-do list, and feel good about it.

Then they go about their lives and assume they're covered, believing the stress of making investment decisions is behind them.

And who can blame them? Investing does feel like a crap shoot, and it's stressful to think about. It's hard to learn everything there is to know, and even then, there's no way to predict the market perfectly. When you have a full-time job and are planning for a family, you don't generally prioritize becoming an investment whiz.

Besides, a 401K *is* actually better than nothing, so Nate isn't totally wrong.

But "better than nothing" is too often confused with "the best thing." Once investment decisions are made, no matter how knee-jerk they might be, many people relax, assume they're OK, and feel financially responsible for having acted. Some have embraced the "doing something is good enough" story to the extent that they've become apathetic about maximizing returns. These investors don't shop around for alternative options. They're less likely to ask themselves which investment assets (or combinations of assets) would best help them reach their goals. They're also highly unlikely to redistribute their investment dollars regularly to respond to the changing market. It's more likely they invest in the first option they're presented with (usually the 401K offered by their employer), or the one they hear about most often. A large majority of "do something" investors have a 401K, and that's it.

Doing something (or anything) certainly feels better than doing nothing, and in many ways, it's a step in the right direction. But investing with the "do something" mindset can come at a cost. When you do "something," and don't explore other options, you can make yourself financially vulnerable.

If you make "do something" decisions with your invest-ment dollars, and those decisions don't help you reach your goals, the implications can be serious. Doing something might be better than nothing, but settling can have serious drawbacks. Doing what's "good enough" can lead to relying on too few investment assets, resulting in gaps in your portfolio that leave you extremely vulnerable.

Take Jason, for example. He's a thirty-five-year-old senior development manager at a major Seattle tech company. He's been working there for ten years and makes $150,000 a year, plus an additional $100,000 a year in stocks. By now, he's accumulated $1 million in his company's stock, which includes investments in his company's 401K plan. However, he has little emergency savings and no other investments. He has no life insurance other than the small policy he has at work, one that pays out a year's worth of his base salary. This would hardly be enough to support his wife and twenty-month-old son if something happened to him.

Jason is loyal to his company's stock because he doesn't think it will ever decrease in value. He believes this because he is personally involved in developing game-changing innovations for his company. He knows what's on the horizon, and the future looks bright. Jason isn't the only person at his company who believe this, so his investment strategy doesn't seem unwise to him.

But Jason hasn't explored other options. He assumes the performance of his investments is almost exclusively tied to the innovative products that emerge from his company, when in reality, many forces influence fluctuations in the market. Many of them have to do with events outside of Jason's company. His stock is looking great, but it's dangerous to think it will always stay this way. There's no telling for sure. Even though his investment portfolio feels great to him, just a little extra effort could make it much safer.

I recommended Jason increase his life insurance so his earnings will be there in case something happens. His response? "I'm not dying anytime soon," and "my wife will be just fine." Besides, his company has already given him a $250K life insurance policy, which he believes is good enough. Even though that policy ends with his employment (which might end one day), and signing up for additional coverage could set his family up with a million dollars tax-free, he doesn't see the need to explore. He's taken what his company has given him and stopped there.

He's done something, and that something looks good. To him, that's enough.

When I told Jason he's better off spreading his investments over a number of different assets, he was skeptical. "Why should I do that," he said, "when what I'm doing is working just fine?" I told him having a plan for the "what if's" in life can increase the likelihood of his assets being protected in an uncertain market. His response was, "I'm young enough, and I'm a risk taker."

Taking risks is one thing; being reckless is another. Risk-taking often involves caution and careful planning, and the most successful risk-takers are *calculated* risk takers.[80] They do their research, take small steps, and prepare for all contingencies. Risk enters the picture because the environment is uncertain, much like the stock market is uncertain. Betting it all on one stock is not being risky—it's being foolhardy.

Preparing for "what-if's" is something calculated risk-takers do. A risk management solution with built-in protections could actually give Jason the confidence to take more risks and more often. By implementing this kind of strategy, Jason could harvest gains, protect the wealth he accumulates, have extra money available to him at a moment's notice, and be secure in the fact that his family would be amply taken care of if he were to pass away. And unfortunately, some people do unexpectedly pass away while they're young.

If Jason took some time to think about it, he'd realize his plan has gaps. And if he doesn't do the right things, he could lose it all. If his company's stock value drops (which has been known to happen), his wealth and income could drop in an instant, especially if the market drops dramatically. If Jason passed away, his wife would only have enough for one year of living expenses, given her current lifestyle. She might eventually be forced to raid his 401K and stocks, which would only give her two more years of income.

Still, for Jason, his investment strategy is good enough.

The "Do Something" Mindset Can Lead to Missed Opportunities and Apathetic Decision-Making

Doing something might make you feel better than if you're doing nothing. But in the longer run, this mindset leads to doing nothing down the road and leaving money on the table. The "do something" mindset and the belief that doing something is good enough is a pre-condition to apathetic investing. And apathetic investing can lead to "set-it-and-leave-it" behavior.

Roger is in his mid-forties. He started out as a product developer at a major tech company, engineering some of the most innovative technology products around. He's risen to Chief Technical Officer at one of the best-known streaming entertainment companies in the world. He has a really good income and a beautiful house in an upscale neighborhood, where he lives with his wife and daughter. His fascination with technology leads him to purchase the latest tech gadgets as soon as they're released, no matter how expensive they are. He owns the most expensive tech-forward automobile on the market, and his home is equipped with the latest voice-activated technology.

Roger has investments, but to him, investing is no fun. Technology is fun, and his job in the technology sector is fun. He thinks these things are fun because there's certainty in them. There's always an answer. As long as you work hard enough to solve a problem, the solution will come, and it will be clear. The stock market is the opposite of engineering: it's messy, uncertain, and hard to understand. So Roger doesn't like to think about it. He has investments, but if you were to press him as to what they are, he won't tell you. Not because he doesn't know, but because he hates thinking about investing.

Roger feels like he's covered. Why? Because according to him, he's following what he considers a tried-and-true investment strategy: invest in some big companies, and then leave the investments alone. According to Roger, investing is just about choosing companies that are stable (the ones that probably won't change much in their value over time), and then waiting for the market to do its thing, which is to grow your earnings. Roger believes by the time he's ready to retire, he'll have what he needs to be OK. In his mind, he's done his job. He's done something, and now he just has to wait for that something to pay off.

However, Roger isn't thinking about uncertainty. Although stocks generally do increase in value over the long term and tech stocks have performed better recently, nothing is predictable. No one predicted COVID-19 or the impact it would have on our society and economy. The tech sector hasn't been hit as hard as, say, the hospitality sector, but an equally unpredictable occurrence could cause tech stocks to tank, too.

Generally, over the long term, the market recovers from recession, but the timing of each recession and recovery is critical. If Roger retires during an economic boom, he'll be fine. But if his retirement coincides with a recession, he might not be. Many people thought they were poised to retire comfortably in 2007, because they did something and then "set-it-and-left-it." They ended up in dire straits when the market took a hit after the stock market crashed, however. Why? They assumed the market would increase over time, which it does, but they didn't consider it might take a huge dip right when they needed their money the most.

People like Roger need a strategy that prepares for all contingencies. A "do something" then "leave it alone" approach doesn't prepare you for much at all.

When All You Want Is to Do *Something*, You're More Vulnerable to the Hard Sell

People who prefer to just do something don't generally do a lot of research. They don't carefully weigh the pros and cons of multiple options. They're happy with almost anything, which means they're less discriminating when it comes to new information. This also means they're more susceptible to pitches made by sales-oriented investment planners with their own selfish interests in mind.

There are different types of salespeople out there, and some are less trustworthy than others. Generally speaking, if you don't do your research before purchasing any product, it's safe to say you're not well-informed about what a high-quality product looks like, what a good price point is, or anything else that matters. You're essentially a blank slate when you start shopping. Any information you hear can't be cross-checked against what you already know, because you don't know much. You're more likely to just accept what you hear.

And if you're listening to a dishonest or self-serving sales-person, you're more likely to be duped.

For example, Jaimie decided to hire an investment plan-ner to help her manage her money. She made this decision after she went to dinner with some friends. She realized over the course of the conversation she was the only one among them who wasn't investing, and this stressed her out. She felt she had to act immediately, or she'd fall even farther behind. She didn't attempt to learn about investing before she started looking for an advisor. She didn't want to take the time, and it was the advisor's job to choose the right plan for her, anyway. She wasn't sure what made an investment planner good at their job, and she didn't bother to investigate. She asked a couple of people for recommendations and settled on the first advisor who called her back.

When she met with this advisor, he laid out an investment plan that involved a heavy contribution to retirement accounts. She asked why he thought retirement accounts were right for her, and he gave her an answer that sounded good. She was anxious to just do something. Based on the investment planner's body language and energy, Jaimie was convinced he knew what he was talking about. Or at least that he knew enough to get her started. As far as she was concerned, the sooner she started doing something, the better.

She agreed to his plan and didn't look back.

Years later, Jaimie had dinner with one of her friends, and the conversation turned to investing. Feeling confident that she was OK because she was doing *something*, she mentioned that she was investing heavily in retirement accounts. Her friend warned her that she may not want to put all her eggs in one basket, and that diversifying a bit more might better protect her. This left Jaimie more stressed than she was before. Realizing she'd sunk so much money into what suddenly seemed like a bad idea, she reached out to her advisor. It was only then she realized he worked at a firm that only managed retirement accounts. In her attempt to act quickly and do something, she made a decision to trust someone without exploring the rationale behind his decision. With a little more patience and diligence, she could have avoided the distress of sinking so much into a plan that wasn't aligned with her goals.

Here's another example. One of the most convincing pitches I've heard from investment companies is that index funds are always superior to managed funds. This pitch is convincing for a few reasons. First, the historical performance of index funds generally supports this notion, especially over the long term. An index fund is a type of mutual fund with a portfolio constructed to match or track the components of a market index, such as the Standard & Poor's 500 Index (S&P 500). Index mutual funds are said to provide broad market exposure and low portfolio turnover. When the performance of portfolios handled by money managers is compared to that of index funds, index funds almost always come out ahead.

The index fund pitch is also convincing because index funds have low operating expenses—they operate with little to no human oversight. While some stocks in an index fund portfolio can tank, others can do really well. What you're left with is the average performance of all the individual stocks, which ends up being pretty good, given you don't have to pay someone for their time and energy to constantly optimize your portfolio. It's the ultimate set-it-and-leave-it approach, and it's cheaper because you're not paying for anyone's time. Index fund pitches are also appealing because they're supported by well-known successful investors. When Warren Buffet and other billionaires claim index funds are the best way to go, it's hard to argue.

But reality is not this simple. There is no one investment solution that wins all the time, and though index funds generally come out ahead, analysts have determined that in a volatile market, they can under-perform relative to managed funds. This is because when the market is inefficient, it also becomes less predictable: volatility can cause stocks to be mispriced, often at lower prices than what they are worth. Good money managers can make the most of these inefficiencies and leverage them for gains by regularly and actively identifying lower cost, mispriced assets, and investing in them before other investors catch on. Once others notice the inefficiency, they'll buy, too, and then the value of those assets increase, reaping gains for the money managers who got in early.

Also, some active managers can potentially see a good deal before most others do. You might pay higher fees for an active manager, but those higher fees may come with additional opportunities for growth in your portfolio—and with less risk.

It's worth noting that some investment firms will tout the value of an index fund because it's a lower-cost alternative for *them*. It's an investment solution that requires little work on their part. Besides, with each automatic readjustment or rebalancing of your index fund, you may be charged a micro-transaction fee, and those can add up. This means that by doing little to no work, a financial planner who sells you an index fund can cash in quite a bit, relative to the attention they give you. It's a win for them. But this doesn't mean it's always a win for you.

This isn't to say that one should abandon index funds altogether. I don't advise this, either. Rather, don't quickly accept an index fund as the best option because it's the first (and loudest) thing you hear. A "do something" mindset makes it more likely that the first option you see is the one you will choose. The best strategy is to align your approach with your goals. When shopping for investment solutions, if you're happy to act fast, settle, and do something that's "good enough," you're less likely to learn what's required to make a sound decision. This will cost you in the long run.

If You Invest to Feel a Sense of Control, You're Probably Not Making the Best Choices

For some people, action is the solution to uncertainty. Taking action is a great way to regain a sense of control over an unpredictable situation. Behavioral economists call this *action bias*.[81] With this bias, if someone needs to lose weight, but they aren't sure what to do, they just pick any diet and do it. If a person is depressed over a break-up and can't pull out of their sadness, what do they do? They get out of the house! They'll go for a walk or a drive, go to the mall or the gym, or take a trip somewhere to change their perspective. It doesn't matter what they do, as long as they shake things up. A single action can get them out of their rut, and it's more than enough to make them feel like they're in charge of their life.

But feeling in control isn't the same as *being* in control.

In fact, action bias can sometimes lead to options that have negative value, causing you to lose. This isn't just true of investing; it's true in life.

Take Becca. She's hard core about exercising every day, but one day, she didn't feel like herself. Every time she stood up, she felt dizzy. Her husband, Thad, jumped into action, ran to the store, and bought her every type of medication he thought might help. He rushed home and dumped all of them on the kitchen table, and told Becca she should try them all until she feels better. Taking immediate action gave Thad the sense that his wife was going to be OK.

But Thad didn't slow down to evaluate the problem. He didn't think through what she might actually need or what might actually help. He didn't even ask her any questions.

He acted to make her (and himself) feel better, but he didn't actually make her better.

Becca decided to wait a day before doing anything. She went to bed early and woke up the next morning feeling well enough to search online for the causes of her symptoms. She learned that electrolytes might help with her dizziness, so she thought she'd give it a try. She went to the store, bought her favorite electrolyte beverage, and drank a lot of it. Her symptoms went away. Now she drinks electrolytes religiously before and after working out, and she's yet to experience that same dizziness again.

Doing something is important. Doing something quickly, just to feel in control, can lead you nowhere. It can even cause you to lose something, like one hundred dollars in over-the-counter medications that you may never use.

It's no different with investing. If you jump on an investment opportunity because you need to feel in charge of your finances, you're more likely to choose a bad option. I've known investors who've suddenly re-allocated their portfolios after a major life change like a divorce. I've known others who've thrown all they have into cryptocurrency in one day because the value of their real estate dropped.

I know others still who've sold off stocks during a crash at a huge loss. (This includes me, in a prior life.)

Many investors have told me they are comfortable with these types of rash investment decisions because they're doing something. It almost doesn't matter to them what they're doing. They're chasing the feeling of control, when they should be chasing earnings.

They feel a sense of accomplishment and gratification because they think they acted responsibly for their retirement and their families. They truly believe that whatever decision they made will yield sufficient returns for their retirement.

And it might. But they may have just made a reckless move.

We need to pay attention to more than just one or two options and invest because we want to reach our goals, not because we want to feel in control. Doing so will give us less to stress about later and less to feel out of control about.

Don't Settle: Doing "Just Enough" Could Mean Doing Too Little

Under many circumstances, we humans like to satisfice.[82] Rather than maximizing our outcomes and seeking out the perfect option, we only explore our options to a certain point. We don't seek perfection. We can't because it's too hard, takes too much energy, and is impossible. So, we do what we think is enough.

Think about the last time you bought a pair of shoes.

Chances are, you engaged in satisficing behavior. Maximizing the outcome would mean searching until you found the absolute best pair, superior to any other shoe in style, color, comfort, and price. But finding this perfect pair would require a ton of work. Imagine how many stores you'd have to visit, how much online research you'd have to do, and how many pairs of shoes you'd have to try on. You could look for weeks, even months, and still not find the perfect pair.

At some point, you'd realize that continuing to look for that perfect shoe wouldn't get you any closer to finding it. Besides, after trying on about eight or ten pairs, it'd be difficult to keep all the options straight in your head and even harder to keep track of what you were looking for in the first place. In reality, most of us go to a couple of stores, maybe a few. We try on a few pairs, and if we're not lucky enough to find exactly what we want, we pick a pair that, although not perfect, is just fine. We satisfice. Or we go home. "Good enough" is good enough, and in most cases like these, that's OK.

Behavioral economists point to "bounded rationality" as a reason for satisficing. Bounded rationality is the idea that people are too cognitively limited to appropriately calculate the outcome of all possible choices.[83] Our brains simply cannot compute all the pros and cons of every available option, and there's no way to even know all the options in the first place. So we do what's good enough. We stop short of perfection.

Another reason we satisfice is to be strategic and efficient. We can hunt and hunt for the perfect shoes, house, car, or whatever, but at some point, we begin to feel that looking in one more store, looking at one more house, or visiting one more car dealership won't give us any new information. The rewards of doing additional research become too small to justify, so we do what's enough and call it good.

Satisficing isn't inherently a bad thing. It's incredibly useful in most situations, and we make many everyday life decisions by satisficing. Moreover, most people are happy with their "good enough" choices when they satisfice. Research in behavioral economics suggests that satisficers are happier with their choices and experience less regret. People who don't satisfice are more likely to be perpetually unhappy perfectionists, struggling to obtain an ideal that doesn't exist.[84]

Satisficing works when shopping for shoes, and it's not too bad when it comes to investing. Choosing the right investments can involve weighing the pros and cons of too many options, which can be paralyzing. The high level of uncertainty inherent in the market makes maximizing even more stressful, so satisficing makes sense. At some point, any additional cost-benefit analysis or information gathering won't get you any closer to the ideal investment portfolio.

But there's a difference between satisficing and settling, and if you don't understand the difference, you could compromise the health of your investment portfolio.

"Do something" investors do little to no research and little or no evaluation of options. If you make your investment decisions prematurely before researching options, you aren't satisficing. You're throwing your hands in the air and leaving money on the table.

Those who settle are often trying to avoid negative emotions. Research, analysis, and the exploring of options is stressful. It can make people feel overwhelmed and a little out of control. The more information they get, the more anxious they become. They reactively conclude that making a decision (*any* decision) will put all the stress and anxiety behind them.

People who settle make an emotional decision, not a strategic or efficient one. It feels right, and doing something that feels right is a shortcut.

Moreover, because they've done *some* research, they can check that box and feel like they've exercised due diligence when really, they haven't. Maybe they had one conversation with a wealth advisor. Maybe they read an article. Maybe they talked to a friend. They did enough to be able to say, "At least I didn't go into this blindly."

But in the end, even though they went through the motions, they're not much different from the "do something" investor. They're not satisfising. Satisficing would involve exploring options until more exploring wouldn't yield any new insight. Instead, they're settling. They investigate until they feel uncomfortable doing any more.

And why wouldn't they? Decision-making can be hard, and when it comes to investing, it's even harder. And it can feel crappy. I can't fault anyone for wanting the stress to end, and for taking action to make that happen. But I do worry for those who give up too quickly. Their futures, their retirements, and their families are at risk of being worse off financially because of it.

I don't want you to become an unhappy perfectionist. Analysis paralysis won't get you anywhere. Nor am I recommending that you do nothing and give up investing altogether. There's a sweet spot between evaluating no options and evaluating every single possibility. I'm hoping you recognize the discomfort of uncertainty, accept that discomfort as a reality, and work with it to arrive at the best investment plan. And be on the lookout for mental shortcuts that get in the way.

Offset the "Do Something" Mindset with an Offensive and Defensive Diversification Strategy

If you're a hard-core satisficer, it's important to recognize that shopping for the right investment plan involves putting together a portfolio. In other words, you're not just buying one asset or stock. You must think about more than just one asset, and more than this, you need to think about how different assets work together. If you evaluate assets independently, rather than as parts of a larger strategic whole, you'll end up with a weaker portfolio.

Continuing with the shoe analogy, don't just shop for shoes (a single investment). Shop for an outfit (a portfolio). And don't select your shoes without considering how they'll go with everything else you're wearing.

It's harder to shop for an entire outfit than it is for just shoes. Because of our bounded rationality, it's hard to grasp the ins and outs of many options at once and how they all work together. There are many moving parts. How can we remember what works and what doesn't and how everything interacts?

One trick is to shift from trying to recall multiple, hard-to-remember options to simplifying them. Categorize options into *offensive* and *defensive* assets. This will give you the right mindset to make the right decisions.

Offensive assets are for building wealth. They can be designed to earn you more income and returns over the long and short term. They vary in terms of how aggressive they are. You can invest in bitcoin hoping to get rich quick, and it could be a confident investment decision under the right circumstances—like if you're young and have time to recover from potential loss, or you earn a lot and you're investing a disposable portion of your income.

Less aggressive holding vehicles that are still offensive in nature include: an investment account with a balanced mix of stocks and bonds relative to your risk profile; IRAs (both Roth and Traditional); your company's 401K, 403b, or 457 plans; and variable annuities. Everyone should put some of their earnings into offensive assets to move forward into substantial asset growth. It's important to look at your short-term, mid-term, and long-term goals to see which vehicle to use, as some of the above-mentioned investment plans are designed for retirement. Investing in a retirement vehicle means you might sacrifice access to your money in the short term.

Most investors select offensive assets, but then they stop there. Investors not only need to earn money; they also need a plan to protect themselves from possible loss while simultaneously harvesting gains. The market is a crap shoot after all. This is where defensive assets come in. What sets defensive assets apart is that their returns are not correlated with the market. Market performance will have little if nothing to do with how much you earn from defensive investments. In an economic downturn, you will receive a similar if not same rate of return on defensive investments as you will when the economy is soaring. The downside is that average growth from these assets may not be as high as if you were to invest in high-growth stocks, but it can be more secure. So, if you want to make confident money and not be vulnerable to the hard-to-predict future of the market, defensive assets should be a crucial part of your portfolio.

Young people in particular are less likely to invest in defensive assets, so if you're a young investor, pay attention. The advice you'll often get is to be as aggressive as possible, but if things don't go your way you'll be met with setback after setback, and you'll have less and less time to make up your losses. A plan to mitigate your recovery time can potentially set you up for even greater success down the road.

Defensive assets may include permanent life insurance, municipal bonds, savings accounts, and fixed annuities. Real estate may also be considered somewhat defensive, especially if you have enough set aside to keep up with the mortgage. Although real estate performance isn't perfectly correlated with the stock market, a recession can hit real estate prices, too. And the real estate market has a mind of its own, so you must keep an eye on it.

Another smart component of your defensive portfolio involves getting insurance to protect you financially if something unexpected happens, including insurance to cover losses in case of long-term disability, as well as car, renters, homeowners, and/or umbrella insurance. Also important is insurance to cover valuable property in your home, as well as flood or earthquake insurance if you live in an area that is at risk for these natural disasters.

Many investors don't think about these options because they don't result in immediate gratification the way stock returns do, and because, normatively speaking, these aren't generally considered part of "investing." They are asset protection tools, and it's important to think holistically about your financial health. Take into account that your other investments won't amount to much if you are forced to quit work due to injury and can no longer contribute to your stock portfolio. You could lose a chunk of your investment earnings if you need them to rebuild your home after a flood or fire. Investors aren't immune from being struck by an unexpected illness or circumstance that could compromise their ability to save for retirement. Few are immune from potentially huge financial setbacks due to floods and fires, which are increasing at an alarming rate these days. It's wise to be defensive and cover these bases.

Once you've established that you need both offensive and defensive investment assets, you can build a portfolio that will push you toward your goals, while also covering you in case your aggressive tactics don't work. Taking this approach is much less overwhelming than expecting to understand every single individual asset out there. It's easier to identify each asset as offensive or defensive and then balance the two.

Let's go back to Jason, the tech employee who put all of his assets into his company's stock. His strategy is offensive because tech stocks are positioned to offer strong returns. However, they are correlated with the market, meaning if the market tanks, or certain parts of the economy weaken, the returns could go away, and Jason could suffer substantial losses. Jason doesn't think this is likely to happen, given how well his company is doing. He believes his investments are offensive *and* defensive because he expects to make a lot of money (offensive) while also having secure enough returns. He doesn't think he'll suffer huge losses (defensive). But his perception of his stock investment as defensive rests totally on his faith in his company—he believes it will weather all odds and grow no matter what. Because he believes his stock assets are totally resilient, he isn't worried.

But Jason's stocks are *not* resilient: his stocks are at the mercy of the market. Even tech stocks are susceptible to dropping under certain market conditions. And with today's compensation packages so heavily tied to company stock, it would be prudent for any employee to diversify some of their holdings away from their company. If Jason made one simple change to his portfolio, he could substantially improve his chances of protecting his earnings, if not multiplying them.

Because of his young age, Jason has more time than older investors to bounce back from a loss. Therefore, if he were to put 30 percent of his investment dollars each month into an asset that wasn't at the mercy of the market, he could earn a steady rate of return no matter how the market performed. If his tech stocks continued to improve until he retires, he would reap the benefits of those. If they didn't, his uncorrelated assets would have him covered, creating an all-season portfolio with a harvesting strategy.

There are many ways to be offensive and defensive. Also, if Jason wants to be a little more offensive in his strategy, he can take about 5 percent of his earnings and invest them more aggressively in higher-risk, high-return stocks. How much of your portfolio you want to be offensive or defensive depends on your life goals and investment objectives. If you want a boat in the next three years, but you're OK with not getting one, then investing aggressively in high-risk, high-return stocks could be a gamble worth taking. But if you want a vacation home and won't be happy without one, you may want to balance your portfolio more in terms of offensive assets (to get you closer to your vacation home), and defensive assets (so you can still have that vacation home, albeit later, in case the market crumbles).

Whatever you decide to do, an investment plan with both offensive and defensive components will simplify things to where bounded rationality doesn't feel so bound, and the costs of researching all options don't seem so overwhelming. If you're covered on both sides, you're already investing with more confidence.

Exercise: Are You Investing Offensively *and* Defensively?

Whether you've invested for a while or are just getting started, it's important to take some time to understand how your offensive and defensive assets can work together. Here are some steps you can take to do this.

- *List all of your investments, including stocks, bonds, annuities, and real estate. If you currently have no investments, list all the investments you would plan to have if you started investing tomorrow.*
- *Next to each investment, write down if it's an offensive investment or a defensive one. Here's a guide to help:*
  - *Offensive vehicles:*
    - *Stocks*
    - *Bonds*
    - *Bitcoin/cryptocurrency*
    - *Roth IRAs*

- Traditional IRAs
- 401K plan (through your company)
- 403B plan (through your company)
- 457 plan (through your company)
- Variable annuities
  ○ Defensive investment vehicles:
    - Savings account
    - Fixed annuities
    - Real estate (to a degree)
  ○ Asset protection vehicles:
    - Life insurance
    - Disability Income Protection Insurance
- In addition to your investments, what other defensive moves are you making to protect yourself in case of emergency? For example, which of the following do you have?
  ○ Life Insurance to cover loss in case of an accident or tragedy
  ○ Disability income protection
  ○ Car insurance
  ○ Renter's or homeowner's insurance
  ○ Umbrella insurance (to cover home + car)
  ○ Property insurance (for belongings in your home)
  ○ Flood insurance (if relevant)
  ○ Earthquake insurance (if relevant)
  ○ Other insurances not listed

It's OK to Take Baby Steps and Learn As You Go

Shopping for investment assets is different from shopping for shoes in that the value of your assets can change substantially over time, whereas the shoes you buy will never morph into something else (minus wear and tear). Waiting to enjoy the fruits of what you pay for, and not knowing if you'll get what you expected makes it a challenge to know if you made the right decision. Satisficing can seem like a good immediate solution, given how stressful it is to guess how your investments will pan out in the future.

But as we've established, investing just to say you've done something and then settling too soon isn't the best way to go. Shifting your mindset is the solution to the overwhelm of not being able to predict the future, and to the stress and uncertainty that leads to early satisficing. Let go of the notion that you need to settle on the right choice *now*. You don't. You can adapt your choices to changes in the market as they happen, building a dynamic portfolio that anticipates and responds to economic conditions in real time. That way you don't have to worry about predicting how things will go, and you don't have to feel as much stress from uncertainty and insecurity.

To do this well, it helps to have an investment advisor or a money manager. But you don't need either if you just want to improve your portfolio a little bit. If you're investing without help, a simple commitment to revisit your portfolio on a regular basis is a smart move. Look at your portfolio every year, and evaluate the performance of your offensive assets alongside your defensive assets in light of how the market has changed, and in light of your goals. It's OK if you don't analyze your investments in any sophisticated way. Just make sure you're on track for earning what you need, when you need it, while protecting what you have.

Make a commitment to rethink your investments when you learn of a new development in the market, the economy, or economic policy, both domestic and global. Pay attention, for example, to how new tariffs might impact your stocks. Evaluate how new regulations regarding life insurance policies might impact your defensive portfolio. Don't just set it and leave it, and don't settle. You don't need to make drastic changes or always know exactly what to do.

CHAPTER 7

THE "DO WHAT THE EXPERTS WOULD DO" INVESTOR

Lev has been investing for about five years. He's in his early thirties, he's single, he has a good job, and he makes enough money to comfortably make ends meet while still having extra to invest. He knows investing is important, but the stock market's unpredictability baffles him. He feels there's so much risk and nothing is certain, which stresses him out. He used to be too stressed to invest at all, but then he got turned onto watching a popular investment program on his favorite news channel. The expert on the program is dynamic and exciting—he seems to know investing inside and out, and his demeanor conveys absolute confidence. Now Lev is hooked. He knows almost nothing about investing, but this expert never seems hesitant or doubtful.

Whatever this expert tells his viewers to do, Lev does. If the expert says it's time to invest in energy stocks, Lev does it. If the expert advises viewers to snatch up shares of a tech company that's about to go public, Lev makes sure he doesn't miss out. In some cases, the expert seems to be right: Lev's returns on some stocks pay off. But in other cases, the expert isn't quite accurate in his predictions, and Lev suffers some losses. But since Lev knows the stock market is a gamble and even experts can't predict what will happen, he gives the TV expert a pass, thinking that whatever mistakes the guy on TV makes, Lev would make many more if left to invest on his own.

However, this isn't necessarily true. Lev could, on his own, adopt a more confident mindset, follow some simple rules, and do much better than he is right now by following the "expert."

Expertise is an interesting thing. These days, experts seem to be everywhere, and yet what qualifies someone as an expert is quite vague. Many are self-proclaimed, calling themselves "gurus" or "leaders" and using slick images on social media to present themselves as experienced, knowledgeable, and trustworthy. A search on LinkedIn using the term "expert" will get you over five million results. That's a lot of people claiming to know more about a topic than the average professional.

But how can we be sure they know what they're talking about?

There's a rule floating around that was first introduced in Malcolm Gladwell's book, *Outliers*: an expert is someone who's practiced his skill for ten thousand hours.[85] However, I'm skeptical about this statistic. I've known many people who've gone through the motions in their jobs for years, and yet they know little more at hour ten thousand than they did at hour five hundred. Meanwhile, others can learn fast, apply their knowledge well, and end up performing better after five hundred hours than others who've been doing the same job for much longer.

Some researchers have debunked this statistic by pointing out it's not how long you do something that matters but how deliberately you practice it.[86] In other words, it's not how much time you spend but *how* you spend that time. But it's difficult to measure how much effort someone has put into deliberate practice. It's hard to know if someone who's been investing for ten thousand hours has used that time wisely and learned the right lessons. When deciding between two investment planners, wealth advisors, insurance brokers, or real estate agents, we usually only have their years of experience to go by. Which means, right off the bat, the "experts" we're following might not have the right expertise at all.

I once had a client who came to me for help. All of his investments were in the stock market, leaving him completely at the mercy of market performance. He would have benefited from an investment in real estate, given his future and mid-term goals, but he hadn't been interested. He also didn't have a solid plan for emergency needs that might arise.

He came to me for "expert" advice. Specifically, he wanted me to tell him which stocks were hot, and what he should buy or sell. When I told him that wasn't my approach, he seemed let down. When I presented him with other options to leave him more secure but still in a position to earn with confidence, he turned down my plan. When I looked at his portfolio and asked why he selected the investments he did, he said, "I do what my friend does; he's been into investing longer than I have, reads the latest investment news, and is always sure of himself. He's also an entrepreneur and has been successful, so I know I'm good if I do what he's doing."

If you're the type to defer to the experts, you're not alone. Many experts have studied investing and worked in the field for years, advised countless clients who've achieved financial success, or have been extremely financially successful themselves. Who wouldn't want to take advice from someone with this knowledge and experience? Whether you follow the lead of celebrity experts or your friends, getting guidance from them can give you a sense of security.

Getting expert advice can also seem like a reliable short-cut. If our rationality is bounded, we look for answers from sources that appear reliable to solve for the fact that we can't know or process it all.

But just because you *feel* secure doesn't mean you *are* secure. If you decide to take experts at their word, or mimic what your "expert" friend does, you could end up with a financial plan that's entirely off base from your goals. You could leave money on the table if you just follow the lead of "experts." Being aware of when to follow their advice—and when not to—can increase your chances of investing wisely.

Not All Experts Have Your Best Interests In Mind—Doing What They Say Could Get You In Trouble

Blindly accepting the advice of people who seem like experts could lead to bad decision-making. This happens in all areas of life. Just walk into a car dealership and ask to see the latest models. If they know what they're doing, the salesperson will spout out features and options as though they built the cars themselves. This is because salespeople need to be perceived as experts for buyers to trust them.

But they're not always experts. When it comes to cars or other tangible goods, it's easy to spot someone who's trying to impress you so they can get a commission. However, when it comes to investing, the uncertainty is much more palatable, which means the insecurity is real, as is the stress. It's much harder to spot someone who is trying to come across as knowing more than they actually do. Under these conditions, you're more likely to jump when an "expert" says to jump.

Take Tim, for example. Tim is in his twenties, and his only investment is in his company's 401K. However, he makes a good income, and he has about $40,000 sitting in his savings account. He knows he needs to do something with it, but he's not sure what to do. He feels the best thing to do is talk to an expert.

His friend refers him to an investment advisor, and they schedule a meeting. The advisor tells Tim he has about a decade of experience helping people just like him earn more from their savings. He explains that he'll set Tim up with a diversified portfolio using money Tim already has in savings, and Tim can decide how much money he'd like to contribute to his investments each month. The advisor asks how much he currently has in savings, and Tim tells him. The advisor immediately starts to pull together a plan that involves throwing all of the $40,000 into various stocks right away.

Tim is hesitant. He asks the advisor if it would be wise to keep some money in savings just in case. He also says he's looking to move out of his apartment and buy a condo, and the advisor assures him the real estate market isn't favorable to buyers right now. Besides, it wouldn't be safe, he says, for Tim to have his money tied up in real estate because it's hard to liquidate. He tells Tim that by investing his $40,000 in the market, he'd be able to sell shares of his stock whenever he wanted, and he'd have funds available in case of an emergency.

Tim is impressed by how quickly the advisor responds to his question about saving for a rainy day. He's also impressed by how confidently the advisor spoke to him about real estate, pointing something out that Tim hadn't thought about. All this gave Tim the impression the advisor was someone to trust. Unfortunately, by locking up Tim's investments in stock, the advisor left him financially vulnerable. A better approach would have been to spread his money out across stocks, life insurance, and his savings account. Then, in about five years, Tim might have enough from his investments and his extra savings to make a down payment on a condo when the market becomes more favorable.

Why would this "expert" offer such bad advice? Because the expert's income depends on how much of his clients' money he invests and manages. If he did what was right by Tim, he would have designed a financial plan based on *all* of Tim's goals, not just the goal of growing Tim's money. Because Tim believed that an expert knew more than he did, he ended up making poor investment decisions that weren't aligned with his own goals.

Caring Too Much About "Expertise" Could Mean Trusting People Who Have Little Real Advice to Give

If you assume you should mimic the investment behavior of a successful person or company, you could be following the wrong person. Shanya likes to invest herself, without an advisor or investment planner. She recently read in a magazine that one of her favorite Hollywood movie stars invested in a new alcohol brand. A couple months later, she heard that a popular, mega-rich hip-hop artist invested in another privately-owned alcohol brand. She never thought to invest in alcohol stocks, but she was convinced that if two of the richest men in entertainment would do so, she should, too. She adjusted her portfolio so a substantial amount of her contributions went to buying stocks in alcoholic beverage companies.

Some of her stocks did well. Others did not. Overall, Shanya is convinced she made the right choice by following mega-celebrities who have a lot of money. She feels insecure about her own choices and uncertain about the market, but she knows those celebrities are rich, and that's what she wants to be. The celebrity investments in liquor were risky in themselves, but celebrities have enough money to take hits, whereas most of us don't. Also, it's likely those liquor companies did well *because* they got celebrities behind them. Who wouldn't benefit from that kind of endorsement?

Just because someone is wealthy doesn't mean they make the wisest investment choices. It's not unheard of for wealthy, well-known people to place bad bets in the market, real estate, and other investments. Being a good actor, musician, or politician to the point of extreme wealth doesn't make someone a financial expert. Sure, those folks may hire financial experts, but those experts are looking out for their clients, not for you. And for all we know, those experts may not be giving the best advice.

Experts Who Don't Know You and Your Goals Can't Really Help You

Warren Buffet knows what he's talking about when it comes to investing. I know because I'm a fan. But would I automatically do whatever he says? No. Because although Warren Buffet knows about investing, he knows zero about me. And he doesn't know you either. He doesn't know your investment goals. He doesn't know what you're starting out with, and he has no clue what your expenses are. So, hanging onto his every word is one thing, but actually doing what he suggests is another.

The "expert" on TV doesn't know your current financial situation. He doesn't know how much you make, what your expenses are, and how much you need to save each month.

He doesn't know how old you are, if you're married, how many kids you have, and what you want your life to look like. Even your friends who are good at investing aren't necessarily privy to your retirement hopes and dreams, your goals, or your assets. Therefore, these "experts" can easily give advice that's either too general or too irrelevant to apply to your specific situation.

For example, when financial gurus on television give you advice on what stocks to buy or sell, they're looking at market trends and identifying what looks most promising in terms of returns. When one stock starts to move in a particular direction, they point it out and convey that information to you along with a strong recommendation to "get on it" or "dump it fast." But investing is not just about buying and selling. You don't buy a pair of shoes just because they're a great value (or at least you shouldn't). You buy them because they fit into your lifestyle, and because they fill a need. This is true of everything you buy, from clothing, to appliances, to automobiles, to medical services. You should put money into them because they serve your needs in a specific way.

Investments aren't much different.

How can an expert know which investments are best for *your* particular needs? How can the guy on TV know what decisions will optimize *your* life? He can't. Your friend who knows "everything" about investing may know you better than the guy on TV, but do our friends know how much money we have in our bank accounts? Do they know how much we spend on mortgage payments, or on our kids? Do they know what we want to do when we retire? Our friends may be making decisions that are right for *them*, but unless our lives perfectly mimic theirs, we're better off not following their every move.

I don't mean to discount the fact that our friends care about us. They do, which is why they can be passionate and willing to help or share information. But they're human, and as humans they anchor their advice in their own experiences. We need to be cognizant that they're doing this, even as we take in what they're saying.

To make optimal investment choices given the uncertainty that surrounds investing, you need to know when advice is noise, and when it's helpful. Following someone else's lead might seem to work if you're seeing returns. But the best question isn't, "What do my returns look like?" A better question is, "Is my overall portfolio set up to earn money and also protect me? Will I be covered when the market is doing well, and when it might take a turn for the worse?"

Following the Experts Is the Norm, So We Do It—Even If It's Not Best for Us

Following experts is the norm in our society. It's normative in our culture and in most other cultures to look to someone who's considered to be knowledgeable, experienced, and seasoned when we need to make an important decision or solve a problem. Even when our problems aren't that serious, we turn to experts. Don't know how to fix your plumbing problem? Want to make your own wedding decorations to save money? Need to get a stain out of that new blouse? There's someone who knows more about it than you do, so why not ask them?

We like to look for help when we need it. It's hard to struggle alone. But also, our social institutions condition us to absorb knowledge created by others, rather than to own knowledge ourselves. From the time we start kindergarten to the time we graduate from high school, our performance is measured not by how many original ideas we have but rather by how well we can remember the ideas of others. In English class, we had to understand Shakespeare. In math class, we had to learn principles that Pythagoras or Euclid came up with. In history, we learned about past events through the interpretation of textbook authors.

If we go to college, we may be asked to create more knowledge, to think for ourselves, and even think critically, but that depends on the college or university we attend, what we major in, and even whose classes we take. Few of us end up getting PhDs, and it's mostly in those programs where students are encouraged and expected to come up with original ideas. But most of us go through our educational careers learning what "experts" already came up with. And we learn these things from teachers, whom we also consider to be experts.

Once we enter the workforce, we're taught what to do by people who've done it before, and presumably who've done it well. More experienced and older professionals give us tasks to do, socializing us as to how things are supposed to operate. We follow directives from our superiors and learn the nuts and bolts of our businesses and jobs from them. As we mature and move up, we may eventually be tasked with making decisions of our own, especially if we manage other people or lead important projects, departments, or tasks. At that point, we become more of an expert, and others look up to us to tell them what to do.

Respect for expertise keeps our society running smoothly. In many cases, it keeps us healthy and alive. We don't cure our own serious diseases; we go to doctors. We don't handle our own high-stakes legal issues; we hire lawyers. We don't build our own homes; we buy homes that homebuilders build for us. It's part of living in a modern society: we all have an area of "expertise," and we turn to each other and benefit from our respective knowledge.

But sometimes experts aren't that helpful. Some doctors miss crucial signs of disease. Some lawyers fall asleep in court. Some homebuilders don't build structures with solid foundations. Experts don't always behave as experts.

Experts in investing are no different. Some are better than others. Some are good, but they're not always clear about the types of people or situations for whom their advice is most relevant. And yet, because it's normative to listen to what experts say, we follow their advice, even when they underperform.

Don't Mistake Expertise for Something Else

Sociologist Max Weber did some thinking back in the mid-1800s about what lends credibility to people with "authority." More specifically, he thought about what elevates someone to the position of having "legitimate authority."[87] He focused primarily on the issue of authority in politics, but his thinking is insightful on the topic of expert authority in general. For him, legitimate authority is generally unquestioned.

For example, if you pay attention to social media, you'll see that there are hundreds, even thousands of young women who claim to be experts in makeup application. They post videos of themselves applying makeup, teaching their viewers the proper technique for how to apply blush to make your cheekbones "pop" or mascara to make your lashes look as full as possible. Some of them include reviews of cosmetic brands, telling their viewers what's worth buying and what isn't. Some of these women have become celebrities in their own right, well-known for their expertise and followed by over a million people, while others aren't as well-known. For some of these vloggers, there's a point in which they transition from being just another person vlogging about makeup to a well-paid influencer recognized for their knowledge on makeup. Sometimes this happens to the extent that they become influencers, being paid handsomely to plug products.

Why this shift? Or, in Max Weber's terms, how does their authority become "legitimate?" Weber argued that political authority is earned in three different ways, and all of them are relevant to investing.

One way in which authority becomes legitimate is when the authority upholds norms, processes, or institutions that everyone can get behind. The best example of this kind of authority exists in a bureaucracy. Bureaucratic systems are full of rules, procedures, and regulations, and we all follow them. Want to get a driver's license? There's a specific way to do it, and we all follow that process. Because we believe in the legitimacy of that process, we tend to believe in the legitimacy of the authority figures in those bureaucratic systems. For example, the director of your neighborhood Department of Motor Vehicles may or may not know a lot about licensing or transportation, but it doesn't matter.

They're the director of an administrative organization that we find legitimate, so we defer to whatever they say.

In investing, the chairman of the Federal Reserve could be considered an economic expert. You may or may not know who this person is, where he got his education, or what his professional history is. You likely have no idea if, during all his years of working, he ever engaged in deliberate practice to become an expert at his job. He's the chairman of the Fed. We respect the Fed and find it legitimate. Therefore, we find his authority (and likely his expertise) to be legitimate.

Another type of legitimate authority stems from tradition. Here, someone is considered a legitimate leader if tradition or custom bestows that legitimacy on them. The Queen of England may or may not be an excellent queen. It doesn't matter. She isn't respected based on her merit—the British respect the tradition of the monarchy. Because of that tradition and the customs surrounding it, anyone in her role is considered a legitimate queen.

When it comes to learning new information, the media is a revered source. It's practically tradition and part of our culture that people who get airtime on TV are worth listening to. Put someone on a TV screen, radio show, or a magazine, and we automatically respect them, because we've always respected the media. It's just always been that way.

When you watch your favorite morning TV show and they interview an "expert" about the stock market, that expert's credentials don't seem to be important. We don't ask ourselves, "Who is this person, and how do we know that they are knowledgeable?" We take their legitimacy for granted because we respect the institution that presents them to us. Suddenly their advice is worth listening to, even if that advice is all wrong.

Finally, legitimate authority can also stem from a person's charisma. In these cases, an expert can earn legitimacy by the nature of their character, rather than by what they actually know. There are many diet and fitness experts on TV that tell us what to eat and how to exercise. But there are many, many more who aren't on TV and are just as good, if not better. Why do some end up on television and writing books, being touted as *the* authority on health and wellness? In large part, it's due to their charisma. They look good on camera. They choose words that inspire and delight us. They look beautiful, and they have a charm that makes us want to know them. They have that "star" factor. Sure, many of us may do better getting help from the highly knowledgeable but somewhat boring fitness trainer at our local gym. But we prefer to follow along with a celebrity trainer's DVD because of their charisma.

In the world of investing, there are quite a few charismatic experts. You can probably name some of them if you can't picture their faces. Some shout at you enthusiastically through the television, while others calmly explain things like your mom would. Either way, all celebrity experts have star power and charisma. They have to—they're celebrities. We listen to the advice of certain investment experts not because of what they deliver. It's *how* they deliver it that gives them authority.

Take Warren Buffett. Much of the time we don't think carefully about the rationale behind the advice he gives. We don't ask whether or not his advice makes sense, and we don't seek out second or third opinions. We don't have to: he's Warren Buffett. He's charming and successful, and he says stuff in a way that appeals to us. Many high-energy finance-focused celebrities have so much personality we can't help but follow their lead.

In short, we support certain people as legitimate authorities on investing, but we don't really consider their knowledge or expertise. If they have a great personality, we're more likely to think they're experts, and if norms suggest expertise, we go along with it. If tradition bestows expert status on someone, we accept it.

None of these sources of legitimacy are tied to actual expertise. If we follow "expert" advice while unaware of where that expertise comes from, we may end up following bad advice.

If It Walks Like an Expert and Talks Like an Expert, We Think It's an Expert—Even When It's Not

One mental shortcut we take as we try to make the best decisions is assuming if someone walks and talks like an expert, then they must be an expert. It takes a lot of time and energy to vet someone in terms of what they know and whether or not their advice is sound. Sometimes we look for cues that represent expertise and just go with that.[88]

For example, research suggests that if someone grew up shy and introverted, spending all of their spare time studying music, we're more likely to believe they're a concert pianist rather than a farmer. But if you had to place a bet on concert pianist or farmer, your best bet would be on the farmer, because statistically speaking, the probability of the person being a farmer is higher: there are many more farmers in the world than concert pianists. But our limited brains don't do that kind of math. We look for connections that may not be there, and we draw conclusions that may not be accurate.

If someone behaves how we expect an expert to behave by using certain words, wearing certain clothes, etc., we're more likely to believe they're experts. We don't even look at their credentials. We don't consider the fact that, statistically speaking, only a very small proportion of people can be true experts, because expertise is arguably relative. You might know a lot about your job, but if you know as much as the average person who also has your job, are you really an expert?

We draw connections, and that's good enough for us. It's a very human tendency, and it's designed to streamline our thinking. It helps us cope with bounded rationality. However, if we're not careful, we could trust information that's wrong, or information that's just not right for us.

"Experts" may or may not know their stuff. But they are more unlikely to know *you*. That TV personality doesn't know your life goals. That book author and keynote speaker hasn't discussed your portfolio with you. They might speak in generalities, touting the potential of index funds or urging a conservative approach to investing. But good investment advice isn't one-size-fits-all. So even when following expert advice doesn't ruin your portfolio, it can keep you from having an investment strategy that maximizes your chances for success in personal wealth.

The bottom line is, when you follow an expert, you take a risk. In order to make the best investment decisions, it's best to take steps to mitigate that risk.

When Seeking "Expert" Help, Look to Multiple Sources for Information and Steer Clear of Specific Advice or Opinions

When the future is unpredictable and information about

what the markets might do is scarce, uncertainty sets in, and insecurity comes along with it. Experts have a way of soothing the stress that comes with insecurity. If an expert tells you what to do, you're more likely to believe everything will be better off if you follow their advice, which means you can relax. The problem is that the motives of experts are hard to identify, and what they advise may not be best for your personal goals.

How can you shift your mindset so you don't fall into the expert trap?

Experts are supposed to tell you things you can't hear or learn elsewhere. But when the advice they share has to do with an uncertain future, you're more likely to let experts off the hook if they're wrong. No one can predict the future of the market, so if an expert isn't right, we cut them some slack just like we do the weatherman who says it will be sunny over the weekend, and it ends up raining.

But when an expert is right, we tend to give them a ton of credit, as though they have some insight no one else does. In other words, we remember the hits and forget the misses. We hang on to successful predictions and ignore the times when they miss the mark. When listening to investment experts, it's important to keep this in mind. You're more likely to forget when they're wrong, so correct for this tendency and pay more attention than you normally would to assess how often they're incorrect. It's important to pay attention to the instances when expert advice lets you down, not just the moments when expert advice helps you out.

If you're a fan of expert advice, consider shifting your approach from following advice to evaluating information. Experts are, after all, a source of information. You don't have to do what they say, but if you listen to their rationale— if you explore where they're coming from and hone in on the "why" behind their claims—you'll learn a lot and have a better sense of the decisions that are wrong or right for you.

One way to do this is to listen to many experts, not just one. Don't just pay attention to the popular one on TV, the one who's the richest in the world, the one who heads up a financial institute or organization, or the one who's successful in some other field. Don't just rely on the advice of your friend who's good at investing. Read advice from people who are less charismatic, who aren't shouting at you with excitement about the next hot stock. If, as you listen, you identify inconsistencies in the expert advice you hear, you're much better off than you were before, even if you're still uncertain about what to do. Expert advice in investing is inconsistent, making it unreliable. If you can see this, you're less likely to fall for the expert trap.

Experts who offer inconsistent advice may, like you, be operating with imperfect information. They don't know what will happen in the future any more than you do. If there were more certainty about the market, experts would draw similar conclusions, but since the future is a mystery, anything goes. Experts in investing, as a whole, tend to move in many different directions. They give you their best estimation, which is often subjective.

Many experts may focus on giving specific or certain types of advice because they're building a personal brand. With their personal brand, they can stand out, become more popular, and earn more money from TV appearances, books, podcast interviews, and the like. A primary component of brand-building is differentiation, which means experts use their messages to set themselves apart from others in the field. If they were just like everyone else, there'd be no reason for investors to pay special attention to them. But experts with a special angle, unique message, or stand-out personality get noticed. In brand speak, they have a "reason to exist."

When you have a bunch of experts competing for your attention, keep in mind they are purposefully trying to stand out by being unique. The information they provide could be carefully selected just to propel their brand. They may not be telling you everything, especially the information that might matter specifically to you. This is why it's important to listen to many experts. Take in the information they give in the context of other information you get from other investment leaders.

In other words, shift your mindset from being a fan of people to being a fan of information.

How are you supposed to know what to do with the information you take in? Isn't that what experts do anyway: take in all the data, analyze it, and come up with the best approach so you don't have to? Shouldn't you just listen to them and do what they say?

Yes and no. Some experts can only take you so far because they're committed to their personal brands. Also, they don't know your personal goals. They don't know what you ultimately want your investments to do for you. Without a personal connection, they can't do much more than give you information that you'll either use or discard.

If you have the time and the will, an even better approach is to supplement what you hear from different experts with available information about investment vehicles. If you're only into stocks, set out to learn about bonds and annuities. Gather information about what their benefits are, why they were developed, and how they work. You may also want to look at how life insurance works, and how it can benefit you as an investment vehicle. Read about real estate investing, and gather information on what makes a property a good or bad investment. And as you invest in the stock market, don't just gather information about how various stocks are performing in the market. If you're interested in investing in a company, look at that company's earnings, try and get a sense of its future product or service roadmap, gather insight into its culture, and understand its leadership. In short, you'll make sure you put your money on a strong bet.

Exercise: Confirm You're Getting Well-Rounded Information

Are you getting well-rounded information? Here's an exercise to make sure. Write down all the sources of information you rely on regarding your investments. This includes people in the media or the news, as well as people you know personally. Include blogs, books, wealth advisors, and friends.

- *How many sources are on this list? If there are less than five, can you think of ways to enhance your list so there are at least five resources on it?*
- *How diverse are these sources of information? Think about their diversity in terms of:*
  - *The types of information they give you*
  - *The sorts of advice they offer*
  - *Their backgrounds and experience across different aspects of investing*
  - *Their areas of specialization (for example, are most of your resources involved in just real estate, or only day trading?)*
- *Set up a plan to ensure you regularly benefit from information from at least five sources with somewhat different perspectives, approaches, and preferences.*

If You Need an Expert, Turn to One Who Can Get to Know You

Sometimes, the need to turn to an expert feels very real and is hard to resist. If you feel inclined to turn to expert advice, ask for help from someone with whom you can build a personal relationship. Find someone you trust so you can share your personal goals and unique situation, and they can then build a holistic plan that makes sense for you. If your wealth advisor asks about your hopes and dreams, thinks about your earnings as income as well as returns, and speaks in terms of offensive and defensive investment tactics, then you're probably relying on a confident investment or wealth advisor. However, if an advisor says they have all the answers within minutes of speaking to you and talks only about returns, this should send up red flags. Their recommendations may be based on what drives their commission.

If your advisor is physically healthy and has a handle on their stress, that's a bonus. Poor sleep, poor eating habits, and stress can cause even the best investment planners to make riskier decisions. The more your expert is set up to make their own optimal decisions, the better the chance they'll make smart decisions for *you*.

Ultimately, because the market is hard to predict, and because everyone has unique goals, your best bet is to work with an advisor who takes a holistic approach to growing your wealth. With so much uncertainty in the market, it doesn't make sense to take advice from someone who seems certain about decisions before they even talk to you.

At the end of the day, typical "experts" won't benefit from your earnings, and they won't suffer from your losses. If your investment portfolio leaves you struggling, your expert friend, or the expert on TV, won't be struggling with you. Your investment earnings are yours alone, and only you will have to live with them. So be sure to rely on someone who has skin in the game with you.

CHAPTER 8

THE "WHAT HAS ALWAYS WORKED WILL CONTINUE TO WORK" INVESTOR

Danielle is a woman in her forties who started investing in her late twenties. After college, she went straight to law school, then immediately to a high-paying job at a large law firm. Today, she's a corporate attorney with a diversified stock portfolio and investments in her company's matching 401K plan. Since she started saving and investing early, she's doing pretty well. But she would be doing much better had it not been for the recession of 2008. In fact, had this recession not hit, she could have retired in her mid-fifties while continuing to enjoy her current standard of living. But, like many others, she lost quite a bit, and though she'll always be financially comfortable, she has to put off retirement. As a newly-divorced single mom, she also has less to leave her two children after she passes away.

Danielle isn't worried because what she's been doing has worked well enough for her. She rode out the 2008 recession and feels she can handle any other that come her way. She checks how her investments are performing on a regular basis, and she's pleased to see her money is consistently earning for her. She doesn't change a thing and lets her financial advisor do his job while she reaps the rewards. In fact, Danielle hasn't changed her strategy since her late twenties, and because she feels fine, she's not entirely open to other investment tools that could really help her.

For example, if she were to tuck a portion of her monthly paycheck into an asset protection strategy, like a permanent life insurance policy with a savings component, she'd substantially protect herself in the case of another dramatic market downturn. More importantly, her choice could provide a legacy for her kids. The cash value growth may not be as high as what the market offers during a good year, but it won't be as fickle. If we were to hit another recession, a chunk of Danielle's money would be protected, *and* she'd have money to pass down to her kids.

But Danielle is stuck in time. She's trapped in a historical bubble—the one she was in when she began investing almost twenty years ago. And she's leaving money on the table because of it.

Danielle is not alone. Many of us invest inside a historical bubble. In fact, most of us make life decisions inside a historical bubble. For instance, many of us wear a hairstyle like the one we had in high school. It worked for us then, so we stick with it, even though it may be outdated. People stick with friendships, even when they don't work so well anymore. We all know people who have friends that are awful, and when you ask them why they've remained friends for so long, they'll say, "I've known them my whole life!" Many of us have friendships that persist, even when they're not the best for us.

I've asked unhappily married people why they stay married, and the common answer I hear is: "We've been married for so long!" I've also known quite a few people who are stuck in careers they hate but don't switch. I know a lawyer who hates practicing law, but when you ask her to explain why she doesn't consider a new career path she'll say: "I worked hard to get my law degree, take the bar, and then find a job. If I quit now, I'd be throwing all of that away. And besides, what else would I do?"

Sometimes, sticking to a plan makes a lot of sense. In some cases, this means having good follow-through, being patient, and seeing something to the end. In relationships, it means loyalty and commitment. But in many areas of life, if you don't change things like your hair cut, your friendships, or your job, you may be less happy than you want to be.

The same goes with investing. If you stick to your original plan and fail to change things up, you could lose money, which means you could fall short of your life goals. Which means you could miss your shot at happiness.

Investment Assets Change—If You Don't Change with Them and Your Investment Plan is Outdated, You Could Leave Money on the Table

If you stick to the same investment plan year after year solely because it's been doing OK for you so far, it could come at a great expense. Maybe you've decided against a specific investment asset for good reason. But if the terms and benefits of that asset change over time and you don't pay attention, you could miss out on a great opportunity.

For example, when Lucinda started investing in 2010, she decided against investing in annuities. They seemed much too confusing, not to mention they weren't relevant to her situation. She didn't think she needed to invest in annuities because of how they work: you invest into them until retirement, and then once you retire, you get a fixed amount back each month. The fixed amount would be exactly that: fixed.

You couldn't get more without paying a penalty, and if you died before you got back what you put in, then tough luck. The worst part was the amount you got depended on projections of future earnings that annuity agents or advisors would prepare. Lucinda recalled her dad warning her that these projections were never realistic. He told her agents sold people retirement pipe dreams based on hypothetical numbers, and she wasn't about to fall for that.

Lucinda isn't a set-it-and-leave-it investor; she revisits her portfolio every year. But if she likes what she sees, she won't touch it. And so far, over the past decade or so, she's made only minor changes. But while she's had her eyes focused only on her earnings, she's neglected to pay attention to what was happening around her. In 2014, the Department of the Treasury and the IRS approved the use of longevity annuities. Before this, annuity companies created annuity products and then trusted their agents to sell them, which meant these companies could create the products any way they wanted. As long as they had crafty salespeople, they could pull one over on investors.

But with longevity annuities, salespeople can only share contractual facts of the policy with clients and nothing more. No sales fluff, no pipe dreams. Annuity products suddenly became easier to understand and more manageable as investments. While others began to recognize the value of annuities and the importance of including them in a diversified portfolio, Lucinda didn't. Since her investments seemed to be OK, she didn't examine options to make her portfolio stronger.

If You're Not Adjusting to Market Trends, You're Letting Opportunities Slip Away

Market trends can change substantially over time beyond the expected ups and downs. If you don't notice major, permanent trends, your plan could under-perform.

Paul and Sarah are married. They're both sixty-six years old and recently retired. Before retiring, Paul did manual labor for a living while his wife stayed home to raise their now fully-grown kids. They haven't had a lavish lifestyle, and they've never had a fancy vacation.

Paul chose his own investments back in the 1980s. He primarily invested in energy and U.S. equities, with very little diversification. He began investing in U.S. equities first, after his company's 401K advisor convinced him it was a safe bet. He decided to invest in energy stocks after he talked to his brother-in-law who worked in oil and gas. He sold Paul on the great potential of investing in major oil companies. Paul was ritualistic about reviewing his earning statements, and he was always aware of how much he earned. Over the years, his investments served him well and his returns were solid, so he never changed his portfolio.

But in the late 1990s and early 2000s, technology stocks started to pick up. Suddenly, there was huge opportunity to invest in technology and make quite a bit of money. But Paul wasn't too interested in tech. Not because he thought investing in technology was a bad idea, but because what he was doing was already working. There were times when he wished his portfolio would perform better, but as far as he was concerned, things were fine, so why change them?

Unfortunately, Paul didn't consider evaluating the alternatives. He only saw what was in front of him. Paul's portfolio may have performed strongly when he set it up, and his returns may have been appealing over the years, but as the market changed and new opportunities popped up, Paul was too focused on his earnings to take those changes seriously. And because of this, he didn't earn as much as he could have.

Changes In Life are Certain, so Adjust Your Portfolio to Adapt to New Goals

The belief that what's worked before will always work can be a problem when your life circumstances and goals change over time. If your plan doesn't change to match your life, you won't reach your new goals.

Melissa started investing with a clear set of goals. She knew what she wanted her life and her retirement to look like.

She and her girlfriend Hannah were about to get married and have children, and their plan was to retire around the age of sixty and buy a home together in New Mexico. They wanted to spend their winters there during retirement, and spend their summers in Colorado, where they were currently living. Melissa diversified her portfolio to include both offensive and defensive investments. She also relied on a variety of resources for information.

Once she set up her initial portfolio, she didn't touch it. She didn't feel it was necessary because she made her initial choices wisely. Not a set-it-and-leave-it investor, Melissa looked at her returns regularly, and they looked solid. She was convinced what she did was working, and she met with her advisor every year to revisit her portfolio. Every year she saw returns, so she stuck with it. Her advisor made a few adjustments here and there to balance things out, but she didn't make any major changes.

Then one day, Hannah told Melissa she had fallen in love with someone else and wanted a divorce. Melissa was crushed. Her entire life crashed down around her. They were supposed to have children and grow old together, but now it was all over. Over time, Melissa recovered, and five years later was ready to date again. But during that time, her life circumstances changed and her future was up in the air. She hadn't thought about what she wanted her life to be like now, much less picturing a retirement without

Hannah. She didn't consider that her investment strategy might need to change, if even for a short while.

Life was rough during the breakup and the years after, but Melissa continued to revisit her portfolio with her advisor. However, aside from some minor adjustments as usual, Melissa didn't make changes. She didn't consider that other options would prove more useful to her in her new life circumstances, or that pulling out of some vehicles altogether to invest in others might make more sense and earn her more money. She was happy enough with what she was seeing. It was working, so she figured it would keep working.

However, a portfolio that "works" isn't always the best portfolio. The goal of investing is to maximize your earnings to align with your goals. Maximizing wealth for its own sake won't get you far, nor does it do you well to grow wealthy just to buy expensive things. But if you could possibly do better than you're doing by rethinking your approach, isn't it worth a try? If anything, by revisiting and reshaping your plan to address changes in the market, with investment regulations, and in your life, you can optimize your investments. You may be able to retire earlier or leave more for your family once you're gone.

Fight the Urge to Leave Things the Way They Are—Sometimes, Change is Good and Other Times, It's Great

Human beings have a general tendency, under most conditions, to default to inaction. It's true that when things feel out of control, some people have action bias and feel the pressure to do something—*anything*—without thinking things through, even when doing nothing could be better. But for the most part, people are biased toward doing nothing.[89]

For example, have you ever binge watched a show using a streaming entertainment app? You start out watching one episode of a riveting drama, and the next thing you know, your entire Sunday is spent glued in front of the TV, and you've blown through an entire season. You may think along the way that you need to do laundry, go to the grocery store, or take the dog for a walk, but you sit there until two o'clock in the morning, watching until you pass out. You could be caught up in inertia, choosing to do something simply because it's what you're already doing.

Businesses take advantage of our human bias toward inaction. For example, social media platforms select default privacy options for you, and you must take the initiative to change them if you want a different setting. They could just as easily give you their list of options and ask you to select the one you want, but they show you their list with an option selected. They hope your preference for inaction prevents you from changing it.[90]

Investors often stick to what they've always done for no reason other than because it's what they've always done. They default to inaction, to whatever plan they already have, without evaluating if what they're doing is better than other available options. It might seem like laziness, but it's human nature. Besides, there's already so much to do in our daily lives (or so much we'd rather be doing), so it makes sense not to expend the energy to change when everything seems to be OK.

When You Stick to Something Because You've Always Done It, You Can Get Stuck In a Bad Investment Plan

Investors may also commit to the plan they started because of a combination of sunk costs, ego, and stress. The more you invest in something, the more committed you are to it. I've seen this happen, particularly to investors under stress.

Chris is in his late twenties. His grandfather just passed away and left him $50,000, which Chris decided to invest. Despite his girlfriend's pleas to diversify and protect himself, he put all of it into a small company that makes a product he likes and uses and that also has a unique pricing model.

Chris invested because he thought the company was cool, not because he believed he'd earn from it. That unique pricing model turned out to be the downfall of the company, causing its stock to lose substantial value. Chris checked his earnings every day and saw his $50,000 turn into $35,000 within three months. His girlfriend urged him to revisit his investment and diversify, but Chris was committed to his plan. He didn't just put all of his money into this one company; he sunk his faith into it, too. He felt his decision was a commitment, but he also truly wanted to believe his decision wasn't a bad one. If he changed his mind, he'd be admitting he was wrong, and his ego couldn't handle that.

The value of the company's stock increased a bit from time to time, which gave Chris momentary hope, but eventually the stock value of $35,000 went down to $20,000. But Chris remained steadfast. He checked the stock's value every chance he could, praying it would earn for him, but the more he checked and saw its value falling, the more stressed he became. Because of that stress, he was less likely to see the negative outcome of his decision and was more likely to anticipate a positive one. At one point, Chris impulsively put $5,000 more into the same stocks. Eventually, his stocks stopped decreasing in value, but at that point, he ended up losing all but $3,000.

Chris took an incredible gift and ended up squandering it because of his very human characteristics. It's the same sort of behavior that gambling addicts engage in at the blackjack table. Having already bet and lost so much, they feel the need to hang in there until they recoup their sunk losses. Their egos tell them they can't quit, and they keep pushing forward to prove they didn't make a dumb decision. Feeling stress from losing more and more, they take more risk and act much more impulsively than they should.

Don't Rely On Your Recollection to Make Investment Decisions—Your Memory Doesn't Tell You the Whole Story

Investors also get hung up on sticking to the same plan because of the *availability heuristic*.[91] This is the mental shortcut mentioned in Chapter 2, where investors tend to put extra weight on evidence they can easily recall to support their decisions. An investor may look at his portfolio every month and see that he's earning. And each time he sees earnings, it registers in his memory. After a year of seeing his earnings increase, even if it's only slight, he has a recollection of his investments moving in a positive direction month after month. When his financial advisor meets with him after that year of earnings to revisit his portfolio, he's faced with the question of whether or not he wants to change anything. In that moment, he'll rely on the "data" he has, which is information easily available in his memory: the fact that he's earned. This makes him more likely to believe that earning from his portfolio is likely to happen in the future. So, he decides to stick with his current plan.

This investor doesn't ask himself if he was exposed to any relevant information he *doesn't* easily remember, like news about a new regulation. He doesn't ask himself if there's any applicable knowledge he wasn't exposed to but should probably seek out, like changes in the market. He uses memory alone (which can also be flawed) to make his decision. Unfortunately, by doing this, he never learns if his choice to "do what's always worked" is best.

Many investors stick with what's worked for them in the past. If their decision hasn't led them to financial ruin, they may see no reason to change. Even if their decision doesn't prove to be a good one, they might stick it out. People generally stick with the status quo, especially if they have the impression (even if mistaken) that everything is under control.

Life situations change, but as these investors have kids, get married, or get divorced, they don't adjust their portfolio. If the amount they have for investing increases as their salary increases, they also don't adjust their portfolio. As the market changes (recessions scar our investment earnings) and new investment opportunities arise (rules, regulations, and products that didn't exist a decade ago exist today), these investors don't adapt. They may continue to see increasing returns with what they've been doing, which justifies their decision to stick with what they know.

You may feel compelled to stick with things the way they are, and you may rely on your recollection of returns as you decide to do what you've always been doing. All of this is quite human. We all do it. But unless you regularly re-evaluate your strategy in light of your current situation, your investment plan will be as outdated as acid-washed jeans. It still might work, but it won't be everything you really want it to be.

Reallocate Regularly. Period.

If you've benefitted from healthy returns over many years and are unwilling to change your strategy, you may feel like you got punched in the gut if the market tanks when you're ready to retire. Or if you don't investigate better options than the ones you have, you may retire with much less money and not even know it. You owe it to yourself to try every possible smart decision in order to reach your goals, including the goals you have for your family. Don't let the very human tendency toward inertia get the best of you.

Change is hard, but it's often necessary. This is especially true when the change you experience happens around you, forcing you to adapt. If you don't, you might leave money on the table. But once you recognize *why* changing your investment strategy seems difficult, you may realize change is easier than you think. There are ways to shift your mindset and adopt a new approach to optimizing your portfolio that can leave you more confident about reaching your goals.

A good place to start is to recognize many investors don't

want to change their portfolios or investment assets because they're happy with the returns they see. As investors see increasing returns with their plans over time, it becomes more and more difficult for them to justify investing in any other way. But as we saw earlier, focusing on just your returns can be a huge problem.

Consider evaluating your portfolio once a year. When you do, look at how your existing returns are doing. Then, ask yourself if any available investment vehicles are new to you, or if there are any you haven't investigated yet. If so, try to figure out what your overall income would be if you shifted some of your contributions to that vehicle. It's not necessary to do this calculation with precision. What matters is that you think through, or even just consider, something you hadn't before. If you explore new options, understand their rates of return, learn how they might earn income for you, and know how much you'd have to contribute in order to earn, you'll get closer to a better decision.

Exercise: Are You Stuck In a Time Bubble?

You don't want your investments to be trapped in a time bubble. Take some steps to make sure your portfolio is current so you don't leave money on the table. On a piece of paper, write down the following:

- *The year you started investing*
- *How many times you've reviewed and reallocated your portfolio since then*
- *How many times you did research on, or asked an investment advisor about changes in the way different investment vehicles were structured or regulated (for example, how have annuities, life insurance, mortgage regulations, or 401Ks changed since you started investing?)*
- *How many times you've examined if new major players have entered the market since you started investing (new industries, new technologies, new types of companies)*
- *How many times you've asked yourself, since you started investing, whether anything in your life has changed substantially to where you'd change your life and retirement goals*
- *Compare the life and retirement goals you have now to what they were when you started investing. How are they different? If you didn't clarify your goals when you started investing, how might your investments change if you clarified your goals now?*
- *What can you learn about what's changed among different investment vehicles from when you started investing until now? Are any vehicles worth re-examining?*
- *What can you learn about new players in the market over the time period since you began investing? Are any of them worth exploring?*

Consider the Help of a Wealth Advisor or Investment Planner

Wealth advisors like myself can have access to simulations and models that allow us to plug in different scenarios and see what's possible under different circumstances. The calculations are fast and efficient, and an advisor should use them to inform your options and their recommendations. Don't be afraid to ask for these calculations. They don't predict the future, but they can help you make the right decisions.

Wealth advisors are also great resources to learn about vehicles you're familiar with but may have turned down. This can be especially useful to find out if any of these vehicles involve new products, or if they've been refined by new regulations. But even if you don't have an advisor, staying on top of investment news will keep you up to date on any changes that could impact you.

Advisors can also introduce you to new players in the market, such as companies that have recently gone public that you may be interested in. This can be especially beneficial if those companies offer something new or innovative to consumers. Wealth advisors can warn you about unexpected changes in certain industries or predict economic trends that might impact market performance and your investment earnings.

In short, don't just look at how you're *actually* doing as

you revisit your portfolio. Also consider how you *could* be doing if you selected different plans. When I explain this approach to clients, I like to use a time travel analogy: look back at the last few years of your life and try to trace events as they unfolded. Specifically, think about how one event led to another, which then led to another. Now, imagine you could go back in time and start the last few years over, but instead of going through the same historical path, you made a different decision in one circumstance. Now, imagine how the rest of your years would have changed given this one different decision. This scenario has been the storyline for a number of Hollywood films, and you can use it to help optimize your investing, except you're looking into the future rather than the past.

Suppose you keep your current portfolio for the next year. Now imagine that in that year, the market crashes. Or a hot new industry emerges in the stock market, or a new regulation makes an investment vehicle more beneficial to you. Suppose the child you want to have enters the world. How might your portfolio perform under these conditions, and will it get you to your goals?

Now, start over, and imagine taking advantage of that new investment opportunity, or the vehicle that changed in some way. How would your future look then? And if you compare the two historical timelines, which one puts you in a better position?

A wealth advisor can work through these scenarios with you. They have tools available to make these analyses easier. I do it with my clients all the time.

When It's Time to Reallocate, Think about How You'd Build Your Portfolio If You Started from Scratch

You may have already heard the advice to revisit your portfolio each year and reallocate. This involves seeing how your assets have performed and making adjustments so your assets are spread out appropriately for your goals.

It's also important to clear the deck and evaluate your portfolio *almost from scratch* every year. In other words, instead of looking at your existing portfolio, pretend you don't have one and start from there.

I know, this sounds like a lot of work. But I promise you, it's not as much as you think, it gets easier each year, and it will prevent you from falling into another mental "trap:" the *anchor trap*.[92]

Say you want to build a porch in your back yard, and you're negotiating with a contractor for a fair price. As it happens, the final price is generally closest to the price that's offered first. If the contractor speaks first and says he'll do the job for $5,000, the homeowner then negotiates down from that price, but the final price will be close to $5,000. If the homeowner throws out a price of $2,000 first, the contractor will negotiate up from there, and the final price will be close to $2,000. If the anchor price is high, the final price will likely be high. If the anchor is low, the final price will be likely low. This is for the same job, involving the same people negotiating.

With investing, when you evaluate your portfolio based on earnings you already see, you're likely to see those earnings as an anchor. If you've earned $20,000 over the past year, you'll think $25,000 is pretty good, and $30,000 is great. If you determine that by re-allocating across investments you already have, you could end up with between $25,000 and $30,000 in the next year, you might be happy. But what if this range is much lower than what you could possibly earn? What if you pretended you had no portfolio at all, and you had no earnings to anchor the performance of your investments?

What if you created a new portfolio from scratch given changes in your life, the market, or investment vehicles, without an eye toward your current earnings at all? This approach will allow you to look at your investment options and projected earnings without an anchor to bias you. You may discover that certain changes in your portfolio could potentially yield more than $30,000. Or you may still earn the same amount, but you could have a portfolio that's much less risky, and hence much more likely to protect you in the face of market volatility.

Don't be anchored by what you already have, and try not to let inertia weigh you down. Look at your portfolio annually with fresh eyes to make sure you'll get the most out of your investments.

CONCLUSION

INVESTING WITH CONFIDENCE

You may have heard the expression, "Attitude is everything." Or that success is 90 percent mental. This is true with investing as it is with anything else. An athlete can only go so far with his skill and knowledge of the sport. A business owner can't bank his success on his knowledge of business alone. A parent can't raise their children well with only their knowledge of parenting. Doing well in life requires the right mindset, and doing well in investing is no different.

With investing, the right mindset involves awareness of all the ways in which your decision-making can go astray naturally and organically, for no other reason than because you're part of the human race. Making good investment decisions also requires careful planning. This is so you can protect yourself against the forces and influences that can lead you astray. It also involves a commitment to stay healthy, be mindful of your mental shortcuts and biases, and be aware of how social meanings and social norms can be harmful rather than helpful.

Remember, confidence comes when you stick to your rules. Start now, and don't put off following them, even if it seems like starting now won't make an immediate impact. You might be surprised to see how small changes you make today can give you more confidence and security in the portfolio you choose.

Understand who you are and what you want in your life, and develop a strategy that aligns with your goals. If you're investing just to grow returns, your focus isn't broad enough. Think of your investments holistically as a source of income; don't chase the elusive monster return. Diversify, offensively and defensively, and as you decide what vehicles or stocks to select, look beyond immediate sources of information for knowledge. And be wary of opinions— look for facts.

Finally, revisit your portfolio regularly, and get a regular update on all investment tools, vehicles, and resources. Your options and life circumstances can change over time, and if they do, you need to factor those changes into your portfolio decisions.

In many ways, this advice is straightforward, but investing also takes work. If you're committed to investing with confidence and leaving as little money on the table as possible, you know it's not going to come super easy. But if you weren't up for it, you wouldn't have made it through this book.

As you follow this book's advice, it's important that you put a few things in perspective. First, though it's ideal to have an optimal investment plan, "optimal" is hard to measure in an environment characterized by so much uncertainty. When it comes to investing, the future is unpredictable. It's hard to know whether or not your choices will be best. Don't take on that pressure. Strive for a solid decision-making process to maximize your chances. That's the best you can do.

When I advise my clients, I work to improve their portfolios incrementally. I don't expect to do a perfect job straight away, because perfection doesn't exist when information is so imperfect. With certain clients, I make their portfolios a little stronger than they were before, and I keep doing that over time until their portfolios are more and more secure. Small steps go a long way, and as long as you're willing to push a little more, you'll be fine.

For example, if you only have the time and energy to join an investment group on social media (one with members very different from your friends), then you're already on a better path. If all you do is add one defensive asset to your portfolio, you're already increasing your chances of success. If the only thing you can muster the energy for is to listen to more than one expert, then you're doing great. When it comes to investing, "optimal" is sometimes just about doing a little better, given the situation you're in right now.

Second, though the goal is to be a successful investor, defining what success looks like is up to you. Making millions in returns doesn't necessarily mean success, especially if those millions are tied up in vulnerable, aggressive, offense-only stocks. Making a choice to please a friend or family member also doesn't equate to success. Even if your returns are strong, for all you know, you could be doing better.

If you want to be a successful investor and not leave money on the table, you have to stay true to yourself. You can't let money matter more than your happiness. You can't let the size of your returns have more value than the goals or dreams you have in life. Money is a tool to get you closer to where you want to be, and investing can help you get there.

If you can get closer to your goals, then you're successful. What those goals are is entirely up to you.

Third, be gentle with yourself. This book talks about shifting your mindset like it's an easy thing to do. It's not. Willpower alone is not enough to get you into the right frame of mind.

Adopting the right mindset takes practice and patience. It requires constant self-reminding. If you stick with it, you'll find yourself learning and growing over time and obtaining true financial health and confidence. Just as your portfolio is a living work in progress, so is your mindset. Work on it every day, even in little ways, and eventually you'll find yourself in the right place.

No matter how hard you work at making optimal decisions, you'll have regrets. But be sure you distinguish regrets over the avoidable from regrets over choices you would've made differently had you known more. Hindsight is always perfect.[93] You probably didn't have all the information you have now when you made decisions in the past.

The best way to evaluate the quality of your decisions is to recall the conditions that surrounded the decision *when you made it*, including the information you had. If you recognize you were swayed by a decision-making pitfall, make a note of it and try to avoid it next time.

I have regrets from time to time. Like you, I'm human. But I'm a far cry from that guy who sat on the beach in Thailand. That guy was doing his best, and he had no intention of failing. But *this* guy is much more aware of how things can go wrong and much less blindsided or devastated when things don't go as expected. Preparing for as many contingencies as possible, letting go of my ego, and injecting myself with a healthy dose of radical mindfulness have given me confidence for investing. It's not easy, but it's always worth it.

I'm not a billionaire, and I probably won't retire as early as I'd like to. My dream of setting my son up to never worry about money may not become a reality. But I'm secure, and that means everything in an insecure world.

I wish financial security for you, too. The kind that comes from covering your bases and having the right mindset. You don't have a crystal ball, but you do have the personal power to make decisions with true confidence.

In so many ways, that confidence is all you need.

ABOUT THE AUTHORS

Tony Sablan, MBA

Tony is one of the top financial advisors in the Pacific Northwest area. He has worked with business owners, dentists, physicians, closely-held businesses, and employees from large software, technology, and aerospace companies. Tony helps people grow and protect their money using defensive and offensive strategies, uncovering pain points in financial plans and offering solutions tailored to every client's personal situation. His holistic approach to wealth management ensures overall wellness for his clients. Learn more about Tony at www.tonysablan.com.

Nika Kabiri, JD, PhD

Nika has spent twenty plus years studying how people make decisions in a variety of contexts, including society, consumerism, business, and politics. A social scientist by training, Nika draws insights from multiple disciplines such as psychology, behavioral economics, medicine, philosophy, sociology, anthropology, and political science to help people make better decisions and effectively influence the decisions of others. Nika has a PhD in Sociology from the University of Washington, and a JD from the University of Texas. She teaches Decision Science at the University of Washington, and is founder and owner of Kabiri Consulting, LLC, where she uses Decision Science to help businesses grow. Learn more about Nika and her thoughts on decision-making at www.nikakabiri.com.

REFERENCES

1   Richard L. Henshel and William Johnston, "The Emergence of Bandwagon Effects: A Theory," *The Sociological Quarterly* 28, no. 4 (1987): 493-511, https://doi.org/10.1111/j.1533-8525.1987. tb00308.x.

2   Howlett Jonathon and Paulus Martin, "Decision-Making Dysfunctions of Counterfactuals in Depression: Who Might I have Been?" *Frontiers in Psychiatry* 4 (2013): 143, DOI: 10.3389/fpsyt.2013.00143.

3   Kathleen D. Vohs, et. al., "Making Choices Impairs Subsequent Self-Control: A Limited Resource Account of Decision Making, Self-Regulation, and Active Initiative," *Journal of Personality and Social Psychology* 94 (2008): 883–898, DOI: 10.1037/0022-3514.94.5.883.

4   Richard Selten, "What is Bounded Rationality?" in *Bounded Rationality: The Adaptive Toolbox*, ed. Gerd Gigerenzer and Reinhard Selten (Cambridge, Massachusettes: MIT Press, 2002), 13-36.

5   Philip E. Tetlock and Dan Gardner, *Superforecasting: The Art and Science of Prediction*, (New York: Crown Publishers, 2015), 35-37.

6   Daniel Kahneman, *Thinking Fast and Slow,* (New York: Farrar, Straus, and Giroux, 2011), 206.

7   Richard H. Thaler and Cass R. Sunstein, *Nudge: Improving Decisions About Health, Wealth, and Happiness* (New Haven: Yale University Press, 2008), 124-127.

8   Rolf Reber, "Availability," in *Cognitive Illusions: A Handbook on Fallacies and Biases in Thinking, Judgment, and Memory*, ed. Rudiger F. Pohl (New York: Psychology Press, 2004), 147-164; Daniel Kahneman, *Thinking Fast and Slow*, 129-136.

9   Daniel Kahneman, *Thinking Fast and Slow*, 85-88.

10 Margit E. Oswald and Stefan Grosjean, "Confirmation Bias," in *Cognitive Illusions: A Handbook on Fallacies and Biases in Thinking, Judgment, and Memory*, ed. Rudiger F. Pohl (New York: Psychology Press, 2004), 79-96.

11 Geoff Covey, "Sunk Costs," *Appita Journal* 63 (2010): 98-101.

12 Richard Greenstein, "The Action Bias in American Law: Internet Jurisdiction and the Triumph of Zippo Dot Com," *Temple Law Review* 80 (2007): 21-51, https://ssrn.com/abstract=939075; Michael Bar-Eli, et. al., "Action Bias Among Elite Soccer Goalkeepers: The Case of Penalty Kicks," *Journal of Economic Psychology* 28, no. 5 (2007): 606-621, https://doi.org/10.1016/j.joep.2006.12.001.

13 Ted O'Donoghue and Matthew Rabin, "Doing It Now or Later," *American Economic Review* 89, no. 1 (1999): 103-124, DOI: 10.1257/aer.89.1.103.

14 Ulrich Hoffrage, "Overconfidence," in *Cognitive Illusions: A Handbook on Fallacies and Biases in Thinking, Judgment, and Memory*, ed. Rudiger F. Pohl (New York: Psychology Press, 2004), 235-254.

15 Richard Deaves, Erik Luders, and Guo Ying Luo, "An Experimental Test of the Impact of Overconfidence and Gender on Trading Activity," *Review of Finance* 13, no. 3 (2008): 555-575, https://doi.org/10.1093/rof/rfn023.

16 Brad M. Barber and Terrance Odean, "The Courage of Misguided Convictions," *Financial Analysts Journal* 55, 6 (1999): 41-55, https://doi.org/10.2469/faj.v55.n6.2313.

17 D.A. Moore and P.J. Healy, "The Trouble with Overconfidence," *Psychological Review* 115, 2 (2008): 502-517, https://doi.org/10.1037/0033-295X.115.2.502.

18 Lydia Saad, "Eight in 10 Americans Afflicted by Stress," Gallup, published December 20, 2017, https://news.gallup.com/poll/224336/eight-americans-afflicted-stress.aspx.

19 Julie Ray, "Americans' Stress, Worry and Anger Intensified in 2018," Gallup, published April 25, 2019, https://news.gallup.com/poll/249098/americans-stress-worry-anger-intensified-2018.aspx?utm_source=link_wwwv9&utm_campaign=item_248900&utm_medium=copy.

20 "Stress in America: The State of Our Nation," *American Psychological Association*, (2017): https://www.apa.org/news/press/releases/stress/2017/state-nation.pdf.

21 Danny Horesh and Adam D. Brown, "Traumatic Stress in the Age of COVID-19: A Call to Close Critical Gaps and Adapt to New Realities," *Psychological Trauma: Theory, Research, Practice, and Policy* 12, no. 4 (2020): 331-335, http://dx.doi.org/10.1037/tra0000592.

22 Mathias Luethi, Beat Meier, and Carmen Sandi, "Stress Effects on Working Memory, Explicit Memory, and Implicit Memory for Neutral and Emotional Stimuli in Healthy Men," *Frontiers in Behavioral Neuroscience* 2 (2008): 5, DOI: 10.3389/neuro.08.005.2008.

23 A.J. Porcelli and M.R. Delgado, "Stress and Decision Making: Effects on Valuation, Learning, and Risk-taking," *Current Opinion in Behavioral Sciences* 14 (2017): 33-39, DOI: 10.1016/j.cobeha.2016.11.015.

24 José M. Soares, et. al., "Stress-Induced Changes in Human Decision-Making are Reversible," *Translational Psychiatry* 2, no. 7 (2012): e131, DOI: 10.1038/tp.2012.59.

25 Ljiljana Joksimovic, et. al., "Perceived Work Stress, Overcommitment, and Self-Reported Musculoskeletal Pain: Across-Sectional Investigation," *International Journal of Behavioral Medicine* 9, no. 2 (2002): 122, https://doi.org/10.1207/S15327558IJBM0902_04.

26 Leonardo Emanuel Hess, et. al., "Beyond Pain: Modeling Decision-Making Deficits in Chronic Pain," *Frontiers in Behavioral Neuroscience* 8 (2014): 263, DOI: 10.3389/fnbeh.2014.00263.

27 Shuichi Chiba, et. al., "Chronic Restraint Stress Causes Anxiety- and Depression-Like Behaviors, Downregulates Glucocorticoid Receptor Expression, and Attenuates Gutamate Release Induced by Brain-Derived Nurotrophic Factor in the Prefrontal Cortex," *Prog Neuropsychopharmacol Biol Psychiatry* 39, no. 1 (2012): 112-9, DOI: 10.1016/j.pnpbp.2012.05.018.

28 Brian Dunleavy, "Depression, Anxiety up 3-Fold Since Start of COVID-19 Pandemic," UPI, published June 4, 2020, https://www.upi.com/Health_News/2020/06/04/Depression-anxiety-up-3-fold-since-start-of-COVID-19-pandemic/2071591283897/.

29 Yan Leykin, Carolyn Sewell Roberts, and Robert J. Derubeis, "Decision-Making and Depressive Symptomatology," *Cognitive Therapy and Research* 35, no. 4 (2011): 333-341, DOI: 10.1007/s10608-010-9308-0.

30 Jamie Ducharme, "A Lot of Americans Are More Anxious Than They Were Last Year, a New Poll Says," *Time Magazine,* last updated May 8, 2018. https://time.com/5269371/americans-anxiety-poll/.

31 Junchol Park, et. al., "Anxiety Evokes Hypofrontality and Disrupts Rule-Relevant Encoding by Dorsomedial Prefrontal Cortex Neurons," *Journal of Neuroscience* 36, no. 11 (2016): 3322-3335, DOI: 10.1523/JNEUROSCI.4250-15.2016.

32 H. Pushkarskaya, D. Tolin, L. Ruderman, D. Henick, J.M. Kelly, C. Pittenger, and I. Levy, "Value-Based Decision Making under Uncertainty in Hoarding and Obsessive- Compulsive Disorders," *Psychiatry Research* 258 (2017): 305-315, DOI: 10.1016/j.psychres.2017.08.058.

33 Liam Mason, et. al., "Decision-Making and Trait Impulsivity in Bipolar Disorder Are Associated with Reduced Prefrontal Regulation of Striatal Reward Valuation," *Brain: A Journal of Neurology* 137, no. 8 (2014): 2346-2355, DOI: 10.1093/brain/awu152.

34 Timo Mäntylä, et. al., "Decision Making in Adults with ADHD," *Journal of Attention Disorders* 16, no. 2 (2012): 164-73, DOI: 10.1177/1087054709360494.

35 Mikael Symmonds, et. al., "Metabolic State Alters Economic Decision Making under Risk in Humans," *PloS One* 5, no. 6 (2010): e11090, DOI: 10.1371/journal.pone.0011090.

36 Vinod Venkatraman, et. al., "Sleep Deprivation Elevates Expectation of Gains and Attenuates Response to Losses Following Risky Decisions," *Sleep* 30, no. 5, (2007), DOI: 10.1093/sleep/30.5.603.

37 Vania A. Apkarian, et. al., "Chronic Pain Patients are Impaired on an Emotional Decision-Making Task," *Pain* 108, no. 1 (2004): 129-36, DOI: 10.1016/j.pain.2003.12.015.

38 Stephen L. Cowen, et. al., "Chronic Pain Impairs Cognitive Flexibility and Engages Novel Learning Strategies in Rats," *Pain* 159, no. 7 (2018): 1403-12, DOI: 10.1097/j. pain.0000000000001226.

39 Nilgun Aksan, et. al., "Symbolic Interaction Theory," *Procedia Social and Behavioral Sciences* 1 (2009): 902-904, https://doi.org/10.1016/j.sbspro.2009.01.160.

40 Yuval N Harari, "What Explains the Rise of Humans?" filmed June 2015 in London, TED video, 17:00, https://www.ted.com/talks/ yuval_noah_harari_what_explains_the_rise_of_humans?language=en.

41 C.W. Choo, "The Knowing Organization: How Organizations Use Information to Construct Meaning, Create Knowledge and Make Decisions," *International Journal of Information Management* 16, no. 5 (1996): 329-340, https://doi.org/10.1016/0268-4012(96)00020-5.

42 Jan E. Stets and Peter J. Burke, "Identity Theory and Social Identity Theory," *Social Psychology Quarterly* 63, no. 3 (2000): 224-237, DOI: 10.2307/2695870.

43 Khalilah L. Brown-Dean, *Identity Politics in the United States* (Cambridge UK: Polity Press, 2019), 61-185.

44 Oleg Urminsky, et. al., "Choice and Self: How Synchronic and Diachronic Identity Shape Choices and Decision Making," *Marketing Letters* 25, no, 3 (2014): 281, https://doi.org/10.1007/ s11002-014-9312-3.

45 Xiaoru Liu, "The Conditional Effect of Peer Groups on the Relationship between Parental Labeling and Youth Delinquency," *Sociological Perspectives* 43, no. 3 (2000): 499-514, DOI: 10.2307/1389540.

46 Eckhart Tolle, *A New Earth: Awakening to Your Life's Purpose* (New York: Penguin Random House LLC, 2016), 25-58.

47 Christine Horne, "Sociological Perspectives on the Emergence of Norms," in *Social Norms*, ed. Michael Hechter and Karl-Dieter Opp (New York: Russell Sage, 2001), 3-34.

48 Jack Drescher, "Out of DSM: Depathologizing Homosexuality," *Behavioral Sciences* 5, no. 4 (2015): 565–575, DOI: 10.3390/bs5040565.

49 Alex Z. Kondra and Deborah C. Hurst, "Institutional Processes of Organizational Culture," *Culture and Organization*, 15, no. 1 (2009): 39-58, DOI: 10.1080/14759550802709541.

50 John Sabini and Michael Siepmann, "The Really Fundamental Attribution Error in Social Psychological Research," *Psychological Inquiry* 12, no. 1 (2001): 1-15, https://www.tandfonline.com/ doi/abs/10.1207/S15327965PLI1201_01.

51 Sharon Glazer and T. Karpati, "The Role of Culture in Decision Making," *Cutter IT Journal*, 27, no. 9 (2104): 23-29, https://www.researchgate.net/publication/293117922_The_role_of_culture_in_decision_making.

52 E. Tory Higgins, "Knowledge Activation: Accessibility, Applicability, and Salience," in *Social Psychology: Handbook of Basic Principles*, ed. E. Tory Higgins & Arie E. Kruglanski (New York: The Guilford Press, 1996), 133-168.

53 Duc Duy Nguyen, Jens Hagendorff, and Arman Eshraghi, "Does a CEO's Cultural Heritage Affect Performance under Competitive Pressure?" *The Review of Financial Studies* 31, no. 1 (2018): 97-141, https://doi.org/10.1093/rfs/hhx046.

54 J. Andrew Petersen, Tarun Kushwaha, and V. Kumar, "Marketing Communication Strategies and Consumer Financial Decision Making: The Role of National Culture," *Journal of Marketing*. 79, no. 1 (2015): 44-63, https://doi.org/10.1509%2Fjm.13.0479.

55 Takahiko Masuda and Richard E. Nisbett, "Culture and Change Blindness," *Cognitive Science* 30, no. 2 (2006): 381-399, DOI: 10.1207/s15516709cog0000_63.

56 Cai Haoxiang, "Singapore Investors—Cash-Rich and Risk-Averse," *The Business Times*, published November 27, 2014, https://www.businesstimes.com.sg/government-economy/singapore-investors-cash-rich-and-risk-averse.

57 Dorothée Enskog, "How Culture Impacts Investment Behavior," *Credit Suisse*, published February 18, 2015, https://www.credit-suisse.com/about-us-news/en/articles/news-and-expertise/how-culture-impacts-investment-behavior-201502.html.

58 Colin Woodard, *American Nations: A History of the Eleven Rival Regional Cultures Of North America* (New York: Viking, 2011), 1-22.

59 Mark R. Luborsky and Ian M. LeBlanc, "Cross-Cultural Perspectives on the Concept of Retirement: An Analytic Redefinition," *Journal of Cross-Cultural Gerontology* 18, no. 4 (2003): 251-271, DOI: 10.1023/B:JCCG.0000004898.24738.7b.

60 "The Heart of the Issue: Emotional Motivators Rev up Automotive Purchase Intentions Around the World," Markets and Finances via Neilson, published April 15, 2014, https://www.nielsen.com/us/en/insights/article/2014/the-heart-of-the-issue-emotional-motivators-rev-up-automotive-purchase-intentions-around-the-world/.

61 Daniel Kahneman, *Thinking Fast and Slow,* 109-118.

62 Grant Sterling, "Gambler's Fallacy," in *Bad Arguments: 100 of the Most Important Fallacies in Western Philosophy,* ed. Robert Arp, Steven Barbone, and Michael Bruce (New Jersey: Wiley, 2018), 157-159.

63 Michael Marmot, *The Status Syndrome: How Social Standing Affects Our Health and Longevity* (New York: Henry Holt and Company LLC, 2004), 23-25.

64   Richard A. Easterlin, "Does Economic Growth Improve the Human Lot?" in *Nations and Households in Economic Growth: Essays in Honor of Moses Abramovitz*, ed. P. David and M. Reder (New York: Academic Press, 1974), 89-125.

65   Richard A Easterlin, et. al., "The Happiness-Income Paradox Revisited," *Proceedings of the National Academy of Sciences* 107, no. 52 (2010): 22463-22468, https://doi.org/10.1073/pnas.1015962107.

66   Charlotte Graham-McLay, "New Zealand's Next Liberal Milestone: A Budget Guided by 'Well-Being,'" *The New York Times*, published May 22, 2019, https://www.nytimes.com/2019/05/22/world/asia/new-zealand-wellbeing-budget.html.

67   Michael Shermer, "It Doesn't Add Up," *The Los Angeles Times*, published January 13, 2008, https://www.latimes.com/archives/la-xpm-2008-jan-13-op-schermer13-story.html.

68   R. Frank Falk and Nancy B. Miller, "The Reflexive Self: A Sociological Perspective," *Roeper Review* 20, no. 3 (1998): 150-153, DOI: 10.1080/02783199809553881.

69   Josh Hafner, "Does Money Equal Happiness? It Does, but Only Until You Earn This Much," *USA Today*, published February 26, 2018, https://www.usatoday.com/story/money/nation-now/2018/02/26/does-money-equal-happiness-does-until-you-earn-much/374119002/.

70   *Bones Brigade: An Autobiography*, YouTube Movies, uploaded May 20, 2020, https://www.youtube.com/watch?v=u4m51vLuwpg.

71   Rüdiger Schmitt-Beck, "Bandwagon Effect," in *The International Encyclopedia of Political Communication* 2, ed. W. Donsbach (Oxford, UK: Wiley-Blackwell, 2008), 308-310.

72   Vulcan Dogan, "Why Do People Experience the Fear of Missing Out (FoMO)? Exposing the Link Between the Self and the FoMO Through Self-Construal," *Journal of Cross-Cultural Psychology* 50, no. 4 (2019): 524-538, https://doi.org/10.1177%2F0022022119839145.

73   Abigail E. Dempsey, et. al., "Fear of Missing Out (FoMO) and Rumination Mediate Relations between Social Anxiety and Problematic Facebook Use," *Addictive Behaviors Reports* 9 (2019): 1-7, https://doi.org/10.1016/j.abrep.2018.100150.

74   Neeru Paharia, et. al., "The Underdog Effect: The Marketing of Disadvantage and Determination through Brand Biography," *Journal of Consumer Research* 37, no. 5 (2011): 775-790, https://doi.org/10.1086/656219.

75   Stanley Lieberson, *A Matter of Taste* (New Haven: Yale University Press, 2000), 14-15.

76   Daniel W. Fleitas, "Bandwagon and Underdog Effects in Minimal-Information Elections," American Political Science Review 65, no. 2 (1971): 434-438, DOI: 10.2307/1954459.

77   Magdalena Obermaier, Thomas Koch, and Christian Baden, "Everybody Follows the Crowd? Effects of Opinion Polls and Past Election Results on Electoral Preferences," *Journal of Media Psychology* 29, no. 2 (2017): 1-12, https://doi.org/10.1027/1864-1105/a000160.

78 Richard H. Thaler and Cass R. Sunstein, *Nudge: Improving Decisions About Health, Wealth, And Happiness* (New Haven: Yale University Press, 2008), 65-66.

79 Michele Wick, "Safety in Numbers: Fear fosters a desire for fellowship," *Psychology Today*, published July 16, 2013, https://www.psychologytoday.com/us/blog/anthropocene-mind/201307/safety-in-numbers.

80 Paul B. Brown, "Entrepreneurs are 'Calculated' Risk Takers—The Word That Can Be The Difference Between Failure and Success," *Forbes*, published November 6, 2013, https://www.forbes.com/sites/actiontrumpseverything/2013/11/06/entrepreneurs-are-not-risk-takers-they-are-calculated-risk-takers-that-one-additional-word-can-be-the-difference-between-failure-and-success/ - f986c383e140.

81 Michael Bar-Eli, et. al., "Action Bias Among Elite Soccer Goalkeepers: The Case of Penalty Kicks," *Journal of Economic Psychology* 28, no. 5 (2007): 606-621, https://doi.org/10.1016/j.joep.2006.12.001.

82 Michael Slote, "Two Views of Satisficing," in *Satisficing and Maximizing: Moral Theorists on Practical Reason,* ed. Michael Byran (Cambridge: Cambridge University Press, 2009), 14-29.

83 Richard Selten, "What is Bounded Rationality?" in *Bounded Rationality: The Adaptive Toolbox,* ed. Gerd Gigerenzer and Reinhard Selten (Cambridge, Mass: MIT Press, 2002), 13-36.

84 B. Schwartz, et. al., "Maximizing Versus Satisficing: Happiness Is a Matter of Choice," *Journal of Personality and Social Psychology* 83, no. 5 (2002): 1178–1197, https://doi.org/10.1037/0022-3514.83.5.1178.

85 Malcolm Gladwell, *Outliers* (New York: Little, Brown, and Company, 2008), 35-68.

86 David Z. Hambrick, et. al., "Accounting for Expert Performance: The Devil Is in the Details," *Intelligence* 45 (2014): 112–114, http://dx.doi.org/10.1016/j.intell.2014.01.007.

87 Max Weber, *Economy and Society: An Outline of Interpretive Sociology, Volume One* (Berkeley: University of California Press, 1978), 212-245.

88 Karl H. Teigen, "Judgments by Representativeness" in *Cognitive Illusions: A Handbook on Fallacies and Biases in Thinking, Judgment, and Memory,* ed. Rudiger F. Pohl (New York: Psychology Press, 2004), 165-182.

89 Christopher J. Anderson, "The Psychology of Doing Nothing: Forms of Decision Avoidance Result from Reason and Emotion," *Psychological Bulletin* 129, no. 1 (2003): 139-167, https://doi.org/10.1037/0033-2909.129.1.139.

90 Richard H. Thaler and Cass R. Sunstein, *Nudge: Improving Decisions About Health, Wealth, And Happiness* (New Haven: Yale University Press, 2008), 85-89.

91 Rolf Reber, "Availability," in *Cognitive Illusions: A Handbook on Fallacies and Biases in Thinking, Judgment, and Memory,* ed. Rudiger F. Pohl (New York: Psychology Press, 2004), 147-164.

92 Adrian Furnham and Hua Chu Boo, "A Literature Review Of The Anchoring Effect," *The Journal of Socio-Economics* 40, no. 1 (2011): 35-42, https://doi.org/10.1016/j.socec.2010.10.008.

93 Neal J. Roese and Kathleen D. Vohs, "Hindsight Bias," *Perspectives on Psychological Science* 7, no. 5 (2012): 411-426, https://doi.org/10.1177%2F1745691612454303.

CPSIA information can be obtained
at www.ICGtesting.com
Printed in the USA
LVHW092326220321
682185LV00031B/215